FRACTAL INNOVATION

JOSÉ MANUEL LECETA

December 1, 2024

INNOVACIÓN FRACTAL

All rights reserved. Total or partial reproduction of this work is not allowed, nor its incorporation into a computer system, its transmission in any form or by any means (electronic, mechanical, photocopying, recording or others) without prior written authorization from the owners. Copyright. The infringement of these rights may constitute a crime against intellectual property.

Edition: www.triunfacontulibro.com

© José Manuel Leceta 2020

"Now we have to regain serenity, the great Spanish serenity that so astounded other Europeans in the 16th century. The classic gesture of Spain was one of serenity that strangers called *Spanish gravity*. Against this background, as on solid ground, Spain must be rebuilt so that each person can start his life anew."

Excerpt from a letter by José Ortega y Gasset
to Julián Marías, cited by the latter
in *La Escuela de Madrid*.

To Marina, Kremena, Jana, and Trini.

Contents

Preface to theEnglish Edition 11

Foreword to the Spanish edition 19

Note about the Book 23

Introduction: Navigations, Explorers, and Discoveries 27

PART I. INSPIRATION: TOWARDS A THEORYOF INNOVATION ... 33

MULTILEVEL POLICIES 39
    Satellites for Everyone? 39
    Internationalising Regional Strategies 44
    Europe As a Technological Opportunity 47

UNDERLYING DYNAMICS 52
    Innovation with An International Scope 52
    What Innovation Is and Should Be 58
    Education and Entrepreneurship 63

A FIRST DISCOVERY: Innovation is About People 69

PART II. KNOWLEDGE IN ACTION: LEARNING THROUGH
THE PRACTICE OF EIT 73

Reflecting with Historical Imagination 82
    Climate-KIC: Reinventing Innovation, China 84
    KIC InnoEnergy: Innovative Value Chains, Europe 87
    EIT ICT Labs: Disruptive Collaboration, USA 90

What Does This Mean for Spain? First Results of the E2I2
Forum of the Spanish Royal Academy of Engineering 96

ENTREPRENEURSHIP: Vitamin D For Our Companies 98

INNOVATION: Entrepreneur or Small Businessperson? 102

EDUCATION: A European California 105

Emerging Trends 110
    System or Ecosystem? 111
    From the Compass to the Map 113
    Unicorns vs. Ecosystems 116

SECOND DISCOVERY: Entrepreneurship Is a Contact Sport 118

PART III. REFLECTION: THEORY, PRACTICE, AND
THE POETRY OF INNOVATION 123

CRITIQUE 129
    Shifting Paradigms 129
    A Clamorous Silence 135
    No More R&D&I 139

INTUITIONS 142
    Passionately Curious 143
    Culture of Innovation 146
    Agendas or Agencies? 149

FINALLY: Like Life, Innovative Entrepreneurship Is a Journey ... 153

IN CONCLUSION: Mirrors, Lenses, and Prisms 159

Note about the author 173

Afterword to the Spanish edition 177

Epilogue to the English Edition 181

Acknowledgments 187

BIBLIOGRAPHY 191

BIOGRAPHY 197

Preface to the English Edition

by **Martin Schurmans,**
founding Chairman of the European Institute of Innovation and Technology; TU Eindhoven,
and Maria Garaña,
global CEO of ClarkeModet, former executive at Microsoft, Google and Adobe; Harvard MBA.

EIT, the European Institute of Innovation and Technology, now a well-known innovation institute in Europe, was founded in 2008. The idea came from Manuel Barroso, the then President of the European Commission. He wanted to build a European MIT (Massachusetts Institute of Technology), in which top science was coupled to entrepreneurship in all countries in the EU and with involvement of universities and top-industries. The founding meeting took place in September 2008 at Budapest and I was asked to lead the Governing Board as chairman. At that founding meeting the bottom-line was: we had nothing to start with. Our task: invent the new wheel EIT. Leadership in these first days of the Governing Board was essential and I decided to take the helm. My position: Let us focus on entrepreneurship both in education of students at universities (next to their base study) and in terms of start-up businesses. We, 18 governing board members, quickly agreed. Next step? I formed an executive board to try and build up EIT in a small leadership group. By Christmas 2008 the first draft of the call for proposals in Europe had been written and we agreed to focus on the build-up of three knowledge innovative communities (KICs), Climate, ICT and Energy. Money available 309M Euros, not bad for a start-up, but of course more than 20 countries involved!

What does all of this have to do with this book by José Manuel Leceta? Well, once you have built KICs, you need to find CEO's for the KICs and of course a Director for the EIT main office in Budapest. We found a Director for that office, but did not know at all what that office should stand for; my error! Quickly the Education and Culture Office EAC of the European Commission in Brussels taught us that the EIT main office must report the responsible use of the 309M euros by EIT and the KICs; after all, this money is taxpayers money. My first director quickly decided: "This does not fit my leadership style", and so I had to try and find a new Director. This brought José Manuel into the picture and he became the first real Director of EIT in 2011. Net results: great insights of José Manuel in innovation and entrepreneurship to a level of understanding that did not and could not exist in 2011. Insights that are very interesting to all of us and form a great basis for learning and for this very informative book!

In 2011, with great help from EAC, the EIT Governing Board managed to convince the European Commission and the European Parliament to free up 2.5 Billion Euros for the future of EIT, with new KICs in health and food for example. Since then, EIT has become a cornerstone of the EU programme in innovation, research and development. At the end of 2011 I came to the conclusion that the start-up EIT was entering the scale up phase and I left EIT.

Three years only were used by this first governing board to build up the EIT-start up and get it into a scale up mode! Our focus in these three years: simplicity. A call for proposals of KIC of only 9 pages, CEO's of KICs that lead the 25% subsidy part of the KIC activity, super simple versions of the reporting to Brussels, to give you a few examples. Under the leadership of Jose Manuel, the office in Budapest quickly became a professional reporting office to Brussels and he learned a lot about the entrepreneurship goals of EIT, which today has led to this great book.

In my life, learning has always been the key: cf. My Tao, Lifelong Learning, my biography, https://www.boekenbestellen.nl/ePUB/my-tao/9789090334400. Also from the book of Jose Manuel I have picked up great and essential learning messages. I take the liberty to cite a few of them and reflect on them. "Successful innovation should be made simple". This strikes my heart: Yes and that is exactly how EIT was started, super-simple, but of course "it is not always uncomplicated". The latter is something for Maria Garaña to reflect on in the next preface: she was a member of the EIT governing board in a more mature phase of the board. How to move forward then to build on entrepreneurship? "Put faith in people". Yes, innovation is impossible without the passionate involvement of people. And "Entrepreneurship is a contact sport". Of course fights, stress, complexity, challenges, burn-outs, everything was under the hood of the "KIC" or the "EIT" car. Any build-up of a start up without this, is a fake, stands no chance of surviving. How to survive? Well, as Jose Manuel points out: "Regard entrepreneurship as a journey, just like life". I have met quite a few business and health challenges in my personal life, but I always survived because I regarded all of them as elements of My Tao, My Life. Only by regarding entrepreneurship as a journey, just like life, can you overcome its stressful challenges.

Jose Manuel finally makes a beautiful reflection on Fractals, mathematical objects of nature in which complexity is described in terms of underlying patterns that are reproduced at different levels. This brings me to the essence of the book, "the book's theory". Also the very complex entrepreneurship contains underlying patterns that are reproduced at different levels. I have never come across this view so explicitly, I like it and it is absolutely true. In a start-up company, complex patterns appear, and yes, in a scale-up they repeat again. And when it becomes a mature company they repeat again. So for example never lose track of entrepreneurship in a mature company. And never lose sight of becoming mature in a start-up company. We can and should learn from this and this makes this book a great learning book that I can highly recommend.

Martin Schuurmans,

Eindhoven, February 2023.

In 2012 I was invited to join the board of the European Institute of Innovation & Technology (EIT). Three reasons caught my attention, interest and curiosity to join this European Commission body. The first was that the purpose of this Institute was to strengthen Europe's ability to innovate. The Institute, founded by Martin Schuurmans, had already been working for four years and seemed to have a real entity and a mission beyond cutting red ribbons and photo opportunities and that, per se, was very different from what I was seeing at the time in my role as President of Microsoft Spain. The second, that the Board composition was an interesting combination of entrepreneurs, researchers and full professors, multinational executives, as was my case, and European Commission representatives acting as observers. A diverse board that together appeared to be working in a functional manner in post of improving the landscape of innovation in Europe. And, finally, the third reason that sparked my interest, was that the Director of the EIT was a co-national from Spain, José Manuel

Leceta, former international director of the Spanish Center for Development of Industrial Technology (CDTI). Jose Manuel had landed in Budapest with his daughter Marina and his wife Kremena, a violin soloist in the National Orchestra of Spain.

The units of organisation of the EIT were the Knowledge and Innovation Communities (KICs), and KICs were partnerships that were bringing together businesses, research centres and universities across Europe. That was the innovative and complicated part of the EIT, a real pan European effort to boost innovation: innovative products and services to be developed in every area imaginable, including climate change, healthy living and active ageing, new companies to be started, a new generation of entrepreneurs to be trained. Each Knowledge and Innovation Community had been set up as a legal entity and had appointed a CEO to run its operations.

From my Board seat in the EIT, I was personally very keen about defining success of the EIT and the KICs beyond activity metrics, beyond those spirals of numbers, scorecards, and reports, that many times prevent us from focusing on fewer and deeper i.e. focusing on results based and impactful set of Key Performance Indicators (KPIs). To make the EIT functional and effective, was an art of innovation per se as nothing was established about how this organism should work as it was a rara-avis in the EU. It was extremely interesting, enriching and eye opening to have such different profiles sharing experiences, expressing views, and setting direction on innovation. How scholars shared theses and theories based on long hours of research, papers, and data analysis, while entrepreneurs and technology executives were adopting a more practical approach from the "trenches" seeking profitability, differentiation, and long-lasting survival though maybe rushing too much, too soon into the short-term results.

By taking the EIT to the next level in its mission, Jose Manuel was navigating unknown waters of a new dimension of public and private partnership, with a tight steering on the €2.5bn funding that the European Commission was assigning at the time to the EIT. Setting his team and functional "rules of engagement" among the EIT Board Members, between the KICs and the Governing Board, and between the EIT and the EU, was an act of day to day innovation that had to work within a well established, process-based public entity that at the core had a lot of talent and IQ but also multiple boundaries, rules, politics, and regulations that, as we know, are not best friends of innovation and speed.

In the last twenty years I have been leading multinational organisations in the field of technology and innovation with the aim of enabling the rapid digitalization of companies to serve the needs and expectations of their customers and, in doing so, working with the national and local ecosystems of technology across Europe (universities, training centres, developers, business consultants, designers, marketeers, integrators…). I concurred with Jose Manuel on the core thesis of *Fractal Innovation*. Innovation is simple though not easy at first sight. Innovation requires detail but simplicity, disruption but consistency, diversity but clarity, connection but courage, and above all, as Jose Manuel says it is a journey and a contact sport.

Fractals are objects present in nature that present a never-ending pattern, infinitely complex patterns that are self-similar across different scales. They are created by repeating a simple process over and over in an ongoing feedback loop. Taking the concept of fractals to innovation and organisations we need to identify and decode the pattern underneath these mechanisms that repeats itself at multiple levels of the organisation. In my view, this pattern that allows consistency, that is repeated, and hopefully mirrored by own actions at the top, and that is enriched by feedback from all levels of the organisation, is the culture. Culture is what serves as the underlying structure that is reproduced at different levels. Culture is the "fractal" of the organisation, culture that is reflected as a unique set of processes, values, and behaviours that define the interactions between product, engineering, commercial, marketing, and all functions of the company.

After the EIT, Jose Manuel and I crossed paths again when I was leading a division of Google in EMEA and he was Director General of Red.es, the Spanish Government agency for Digital Transformation. From that time, I remember his ambition to put Spain at the front end of digitalization and always "thinking big" for our country. As practitioners, we used to exchange reflections and experiences about the ability of organisations to innovate, to do things differently, to unlearn years of values, and behaviours, to take risks and to win over the extremely strong inertia of what is known turf. Jose Manuel is a man of the Renaissance in the field of innovation: he has led large public organisations, has partnered, and understands well the wide and complex ecosystem of private companies from entrepreneurs owning an idea to big multinationals, while at the same time, he is a relentless researcher and publisher.

I find the theory of fractals as the unit of thinking for innovation extremely interesting. In the crowded space of innovation literature, Jose Manuel´s book presents an interesting, mathematical inspiration but humanistic theory behind the art of innovation. A great value proposition, I highly recommend its reading.

Maria Garaña,
London, March 2023.

Foreword to the Spanish edition

by Andrés Pedreño,
Entrepreneur, former President of Alicantec
and Rector of Alicante University.

José Manuel Leceta is one of those privileged assets that any country has the obligation to exploit, much more so in troubled and complex times where most of the talent is insufficient. Institutions such as Red.es, the Center for the Development of Industrial Technology (CDTI), the European Space Agency (ESA), and the European Institute of Innovation and Technology (EIT) have benefited from his experience, vision, and capability. This book and its chapters are a reflection of his achievements in professional leadership and knowledge in institutions within the highest national and international range.

In a few years we have gone from innovation management to disruption management, from the strategic business plan to start-up canvas, from the manufacturing industry to industry 4.0 and society 5.0, and from the linear trend to the exponential one. In this context, the author, an expert in the international and especially the European innovation realm, understands the crossroads in which our continent finds itself against the growing leadership of the US and China.

From the beginning he raises the key question, "Why are Europe and Spain not advancing at the correct pace?" His book, *Fractal Innovation,* is a manual that should be well read, apart from its claim to the general public, also by business leaders and researchers. Where still, far from losing hope, José Manuel sees Europe as a technological opportunity if we acknowledge our existential need for innovation on the ground of an international level, combining local capillarity and global reach.

In an environment like ours, where there is an excess of complexity and buzz words, updated knowledge of the theoretical soundness of Schumpeter or the empiricall attractiveness of Porter are being used less and less. Perhaps an engineer with philosophical interests, such as Leceta, is well placed to highlight a seamless remedy where "education and entrepreneurship" are used within a framework where managerial economics is disrupted by entrepreneurial economics. The transition from Peter Drucker to Steve Blank is implicit in the reasoning and demands for the economy in Europe where still today scalable entrepreneurship is absent.

In Europe and Spain there are many watertight areas for innovation. In the words of Leceta, "financing science and innovation in research centers and existing business firms is not enough. Innovation through venture requires talent and determination." One of the keys that is cited in the book is to achieve a change in perception and recognition of the undertaking of entrepreneurs in Europe. We are still a long way from the United States. It is important to welcome a debate that also addresses the role of education for innovation and entrepreneurship.

Another contribution of José Manuel Leceta is that, far from getting lost in the complexity of systems or ecosystems of innovation and complex interconnections and interdependencies, he clarifies rules and clear principles of action. He also warns us about restrictions on many topics, of which there are many to choose from, such as the "no more R & D & i" (I+D+i in Spanish, which captures the obsolete linear model of innovation) whereby innovation is seen as a byproduct of science.

Few things escape the attention of the author: systems, ecosystems, innovation agencies, talent etc. This is a very pleasing read, facilitated by a rigorous style that is entertaining and integrates pieces from Ortega y Gasset, Unamuno, Ramón y Cajal as well as Steve Jobs, united in a kind of brilliant and motivating dialectic.

His approaches and contributions are a good catalogue for political action that includes education for innovation and entrepreneurship, open innovation and intra- entrepreneurship, and radical and disruptive innovation. Despite the complexity of the phenomena that underlies the digital economy, orchestrating leadership to create, compete, collaborate, and control is a good antidote for confusion or inaction.

All that remains is for me to wish that many of these contributions of the author are implemented in Spain. If this can be done with his help, all the better. We need a strong digital economy and a relevant position in the sectors of the future. There is not enough awareness of this in a country like ours, which has the second highest rate of ageing as well as a critical level of debt. During the crisis, the level of debt rose to chilling figure and, still today, Spain boasts the second highest rate of ageing as well as the highest rate of youth unemployment in Europe after Greece. We need clarity of ideas to face this situation. Thank you very much José Manuel for helping us reflect on what innovation and entrepreneurship mean!

Andres Pedreño

Alicante, March 2019

Note about the Book

by Prof. Xavier Ferrás,
Director at ESADE Business School and
Chairman of INDi Advisory Board, Viladecans.

The book you are holding in your hands is one of the most profound, holistic, and intellectually sophisticated compendia that has been produced in recent years on the phenomenon of innovation. The author, one of Spain's greatest talents in policies and innovation strategies, projects in these pages his extensive experience as a long standing public manager as he has occupied key management positions in the technology system, both in our country and at the European Union level. He also shares his knowledge as a scholar and researcher of innovation. But he does so with a broad perspective, decorating his text with contributions from different disciplines such as mathematics, physics, engineering, psychology, and philosophy to prove his overflowing intellectual curiosity and his keen interest in the subject.

This book is written by a Renaissance man. And it is written from a Renaissance perspective also. It masterfully connects points initially scattered in different fields of science and humanities (a real "connecting the dots" in the creative sense that inspired Steve Jobs). The book exudes an old Renaissance essence, which reflects the sharp dilemmas of ancient Greece but links them with an aspiration and a dream for the future: a new, European technological Renaissance. A Europe that yearns to be reindustrialised and competitive. A Europe able to deploy a 4.0 industrial structure that is smart, sustainable, and inclusive within the framework of a democratic and knowledge-based society. That merges the culture and history of the Old Continent with a renewed entrepreneurial spirit and new waves of disruptive technology. A longing, in short, for a Europe that does not disappear from the flow of history.

An original idea appears in the core of the text, with precedents in the world of physics. Is there a theory behind innovation? Is there a general theory of innovation? Are we in love with innovation only by chance because life has led us to work with it or are we in love with innovation because there is something superior, metaphysical and mysterious behind the concept? Is there something paraphysical that attracts us and excites us because of its intrinsic beauty? Is there a type of law that explains the dynamics of innovation in a unique way, regardless of where you look at it from (from economics, from technology, from psychology, from the social sciences, or from neuroscience)? Because, if there is, then maybe innovation is more than an exciting concept of management. If such a superior scheme is true, we would have found something exceptionally beautiful, something like a thermodynamic principle of systemic change (regardless of the angle from which the system is analysed). From this perspective, innovation would follow unique patterns, regardless of the level at which it is analysed. In the light of that argument, the supreme idea that gives the book its title is born. If there is a general theory of innovation, then innovation is a fractal phenomenon that replicates itself at different levels.

José Manuel Leceta provides the masterful empirical basis for this hypothesis. The culmination of his book relates the models of management of the four competitive values of Quinn and Roor-Baugh with Benziger's four thinking styles and the four styles of leadership in relation to the organisation of the life cycle of DeGraff and Isenberg's innovative ecosystem models. As well as different levels of innovation corresponding to different systems such as the brain, the individual, the company, or economy, where Leceta finds the basis of his general theory. In all of them, a similar framework of relationships are reproduced: creation, competition, collaboration, and control. Also, in all of them, innovation (or, more generically, change), is governed by a struggle between opposing forces, a creative tension between the new and the old; between the emerging and the obsolete; between the promising and the consolidated. If we were Eastern, we would speak of the eternal conflict between yin and yang as the basis for creativity and change. The result of this creative tension generates different types of innovation: disruptive, sustained, radical, and incremental in each of the observed systems.

Is innovation a fractal phenomenon? Is there a general theory of innovation? Leceta lays the foundations for us to think that this is indeed the case. As in mathematics, when faced with a dilemma, the shortest way to the solution is always the most elegant way, the one that is formally more beautiful. José Manuel Leceta, this Renaissance man, has brought a new enlightened look at the phenomenon of innovation and offers one of the most beautiful and elegant ways to deeply understand this exciting phenomenon that absorbs us: innovation. Congratulations and congratulations on this masterpiece.

Xavier Ferrás

Barcelona, October 2019

Introduction:
Navigations, Explorers, and Discoveries

I begin the essay, which collects many of my press articles on policies for and practices of innovation and entrepreneurship, a subject that fascinates me and in which I find both a challenge and a conviction. A challenge because knowing the underlying dynamics of these phenomena requires a great effort to grasp the keys of something that, by its very nature, is constantly evolving. The conviction is that whoever understands the essence of it will be able to navigate the apparent complexity of the world a little better. The book is therefore an invitation to explore the regularities and dynamics that characterise entrepreneurship and innovation.

The book is a kaleidoscope of writings to continue on the path laid out by the great Spanish philosopher José Ortega y Gasset, with a small *truth in perspective*, valid from that perspective and complementary to others. I obviously do this from my own experience but also from the evidence of our time. This is so as innovation is essentially change and entrepreneurship is an attitude. My overall view is centered around the human factor (my own experience) but also the social factor (our time) as well. Everything happens within a context and, at the same time, we are all necessary because each of us carries a unique view of the world, a Leibnizian monad.

Both Leibniz and Ortega, are present in Javier Echeverría's *El arte de la innovación,* an inspiring book where he proposes a "philosophy of innovation", parallel to the philosophy of science. With this, I trust that the readers of my book will excuse the weakness of an engineer like myself who has philosophical interests but also a lot to learn. However, since I am convinced that first intuitions are ultimately the best ones and that only challenges help us develop, I trust that my early publications will be of interest as they helped me shed some light on the fairly unknown path I have followed which, in the light of my experience, will hopefully serve others as a whole.

The book is structured in three parts. First a reflective part, starting with a counterexample of my first press article published in *El País* back in 1991, to then look at the evolution of the public policies developed in Europe for innovation. But as Ortega also said human beings have no nature, but just history, I try to organise my ideas so that the reader can find his or her own way to navigate along the way of my own personal discoveries in a friendly and more stimulating way.

The second part is the nucleus of the book, gathers my own learnings at the European Institute of Innovation and Technology (EIT) and reflects around innovation as "knowledge in action". Something that I try to illustrate in historical perspective with the first three Knowledge and Innovation Communities (KICs) that the EIT launched in 2010 against the backdrop of what some know as the Fourth Industrial Revolution and others as the Third Cognitive Revolution. I end this part with notes on how to manage processes, which is, after all, the best way one can do in complex environments of education, entrepreneurship and innovation.

Finally, the third part draws some general conclusions from the cases cited above. First, on an hypothetical theory or science of innovation, if such a discipline could be ever properly formulated and discussed. Second, of trends in practice with new emerging policies for innovation. Finally, the *poiesis* (production), a concept that comes from Plato and Aristotle in between theory and practice, whereby I address important intangibles such as leadership, culture and social conscience.

The thesis of the book is that, despite the apparent complexity of policies and practices of innovation and entrepreneurship, there may be underlying structures to systems, organisations and individuals. Beyond its content, the book invites us to look ahead with confidence, reconquering the potential that each of us has to build a better world and, at the same time, the need to recognize our own limitations and, consequently, our fundamental need for others. This is so when setting up an entrepreneurial new team or firm and I believe this is also for society as a whole.

The title, *Fractal Innovation*, postulates this same vision for a topic that is complex at first sight and whose theory is still being created. Navigating the complexity of the world means managing the tensions and integrating the diversity that any human adventure worth living requires. Indeed, reconciling tensions is essential while orchestrating diversity is crucial to scale up any model of activity. I therefore talk about how to live with what Jeff DeGraff calls *constructive conflict* using the greatness and gravity of which Spaniards were maybe better equipped in other times, according to Julián Marías, the main disciple of Ortega y Gasset, recalled in the first pages of this book. In my view, however, nothing prevents us from recovering such gravity.

The book provides an account of my experience in the management of innovative agencies and public entities that operate with business and entrepreneurial logics. After my professional time in industry, I am in permanent debt to the European Space Agency

(ESA), the Center for the Development of Industrial Technology (CDTI), the European Institute of Innovation and Technology (EIT) and Red.es. They were the places where I could take on new challenges and, through them, develop myself with a fascination about the impact one can only foster with an appetite for change. The book is dedicated to my supervisors and collaborators in these organisations who shared their faith and passion to foster the *Entrepreneurial State* of Mariana Mazzucato, author of the famous book published a decade ago with that same title, perhaps the latest attempt on a theory of the science of innovation.

All in all, operationalizing the Entrepreneurial State today seems more an art than a technique, although for the ancient Greeks and Romans both terms were equivalent: *Techne and Ars*. Because there can hardly be any definitive knowledge (*episteme* for the Greeks) or science (*scientia* for the Romans) about all this, which governments try to capture in institutions and entities: public policies for innovation and entrepreneurship are complex. Daniel Breznitz thoroughly addressed this question in his work *Innovation and the State* which, interestingly, is specular to the title of Mariana Mazzucato's book that I read during my stay at the European University Institute in Florence, even more when translated into Italian: *Lo Stato Innovatore*.

Inspired by these authors and encouraged by my own experience and intuitions in the conduct of my duties in the specialised, innovative and entrepreneurial agencies mentioned above, I hope this book serves to encourage the general public to read about these matters, which today are often left to researchers, technologists and experts. This is important if, as Nobel Prize winner Edmund Phelps vehemently defends, the mass flowering of entrepreneurship and innovation is not historically the heritage of a few, but was an effective system until the 70s when Western economies saw their productivity reduced. Innovative entrepreneurship must be everyone's sport for the double reasons that our future depends so much on it and because it explains much of the complexity of the world at the same time.

In the navigation to which the reader ventures, great professionals who honour me with their friendship such as Luis Fernando Alvarez and Juan Mulet, CEOs of Secure Solutions-GMV and the Foundation *España Digital*, respectively, were kind enough to consider the first full draft text in Spanish and to recommended me tactfully not to assume any previous knowledge from the readers. It is true that if all "science" starts with a good definition, this term did not appear until 1840 to describe what was previously known as "natural philosophy." Also, the fascination of the first pre-Socratic philosophers was due to their belief that, beyond the incessant change of the world, there should be principles that were first and last causes, as stated by Aristotle later on. Without postulating a kind of *anamnesis* of innate ideas like Socrates and Plato, I should point at some firm ports for navigation, moving away from long canonical definitions that are so frequently found in many manuals.

Today innovation and entrepreneurship appear in every colloquial conversation while their meanings are paradoxically so polysemic. Let's set two simple notions for the time being. First, to define innovation essentially as "successfully exploiting new ideas" and stressing therefore, that this requires an impact that does not necessarily require a new invention or a novel scientific discovery. On the contrary, many successful innovations result from combinations of existing knowledge. Second, entrepreneurship means a willingness to undertake something new or "undertake self-changes" and therefore is an attitude not only to create a new business, which is its narrowest meaning. For now, these general brushstrokes will suffice.

Finally, an idea that the reader will frequently find in the pages that follow revolves around the actor ′par excellence′ when we talk about innovation (the firm) and its context (the National Innovation System). This is an idea that runs parallel in the entrepreneurship literature, where the entrepreneur is the key agent and the ecosystem is the context. The Hispanic reader will perfectly understand both realities and be accustomed to thinking of oneself and one's own circumstance which Ortega postulated in his book *Meditations on Quixote* in 1914. More importantly, the reflections on the vital reasons that motivate people, businesses, and communities. This is a subject to which we will return at the end of our particular navigation.

Speaking of navigations, José Luis Molinuevo finishes his book, *Para leer a Ortega,* with an idea that Xavier Ferrás curiously takes on board in presenting this work and to whom I sincerely thank for his example and encouragement, same as to Andrés Pedreño, Alfredo Sanchez and Totti Konnola. The citation reads: *"The way a man is, is society, and in our days, a technological society. However, "society is a collectivity of individuals under the pressure of a system of uses". And it is these uses that confront us with a new challenge, this time no longer a challenge of a dominant Nature, rather this supernatural one that are new technologies. From there, the question that Ortega leaves us is, "How can we carry out the cultural and political construction of Europe in a society of new technologies?" This could be a "third navigation" from Ortega."* This is not a minor issue, quite the contrary, it is an issue whose time has come and requires everyone to keep up with our times.

PART I.
INSPIRATION: TOWARDS A THEORY OF INNOVATION

FRACTAL INNOVATION

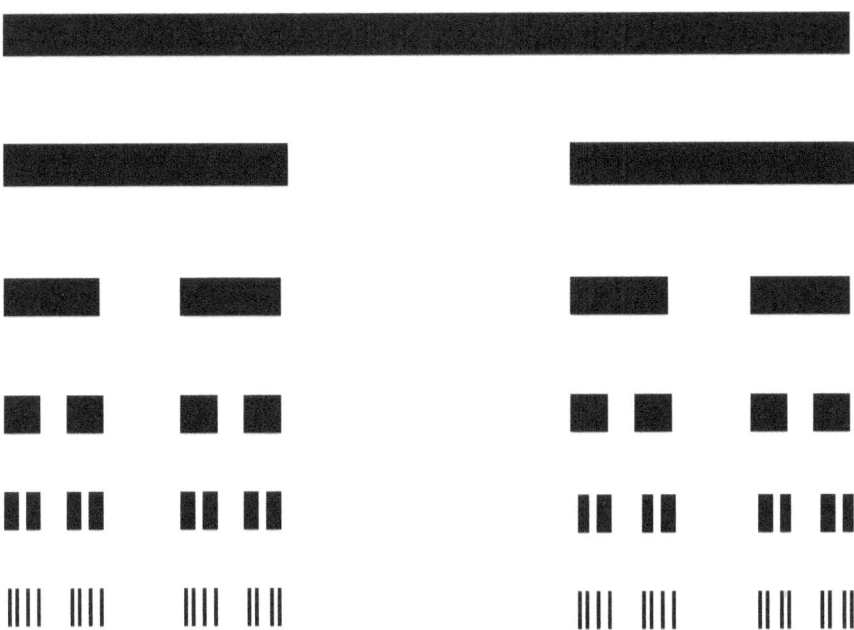

N.B. Dust of Cantor. It is probably the oldest documented fractal and historically the first pure fractal object. It was described by the German mathematician Georg Ferdinand Ludwig Philipp Cantor (1845-1918) around 1872. The historical development of set theory is also attributed to Cantor. This set and fractal can be recreated by taking a line, dividing it into three equal parts and removing the central part, after this we do the same thing again with the remaining lines and continue doing it to infinity.

After my first professional years in the Spanish electronics industry (first PESA during my University studies and later with Alcatel Spacio), I was sponsored by the European Space Agency (ESA) to participate in the Summer Session Programme organised by the International Space University (ISU) in 1991 (Toulouse, France) where I got a diploma signed by Arthur C. Clarke! The ISU was created by Peter Diamandis, best known for Singularity University (SU) inspired by Raymond Kurzweil and his 2005 book *Singularity Is Near*. A year later, I was happy to join the academic team of the University in 1992 (Kitakyushu, Japan) as a staff member.

Taking advantage of the impact that the ISU Summer Session had in Spain at the time and the kind offer by the veteran science journalist Alicia Rivera of the Spanish newspaper *El País*, I ventured to write my first press article. An article that, I believe, has a certain interest and relevance beyond its content, as it will serve to set the scene for the topics that will be discussed later in these pages. Namely, that every innovation is a novelty but not every novelty is necessarily an innovation.

With this we must insist, as did the famous economist Joseph A. Schumpeter more than a century ago, that inventing is not the same as innovating. Neither innovation is equal to venturing even though these words seem closely related and confusing for the general public. Nor have science and technology historically gone hand in hand. Let's therefore stress that innovation is not necessarily a by-product of scientific research, as the latter is not always necessary and is never sufficient to innovate. I trust that these assertions will make sense as reading progresses since, also for me, it took time and effort to truly understand all these concepts.

Indeed, when I moved from the Spanish delegation to ESA to the International Directorate position at the Center for the

Development of Industrial Technology (CDTI), I understood that international cooperation in R & D is justified not only by the critical mass of economic and human resources involved, which is the principal logic of intervention at ESA, but also in the search for knowledge and markets with characterises the so-called "technological strategic alliances" in the literature, including at the transnational level. On the other hand, at the CDTI, innovation was a matter of business firms and projects. Later at the EIT, I understood that innovation requires an entrepreneurial mindset, which ecosystems can nurture. In short, I discovered the human and social factors of innovation.

But, after so much experimentation with the successive editions of the European Union R&D Framework Programme, why are Europe and Spain not progressing at a proper pace? An example will suffice to highlight the commitments and paradoxes encountered in designing effective policies for innovation and entrepreneurship, which once again substantiates the complexity of the matter. Because, it is where opposites intersect that the public decision-makers will have to manage tensions. This is so across the multilevel approach that characterises the European model of innovation policies, whereby European, national and regional programmes coexist. The question is what is the level of optimal administrative intervention needed to match the real nature of knowledge concerning innovation and competition?

On the one hand, innovation occurs locally, linked to agglomeration phenomena which explains public support for business clusters and nearby incubation of new businesses. Responding to the nature of innovation, it would seem logical that funding and policy management are more national and local rather than international or transnational. This is the current approach in Europe where 85 -90% of public funding for R&D is managed at national and regional level.

On the other hand, <u>competition</u> for markets and knowledge is increasingly global, necessitating that innovation has greater impact, ideally new to the world, as well as to accelerate the growth of new businesses. From this perspective, both knowledge and markets become increasingly global and, within this logic, policy interventions should then be less national/local and more international/transnational.

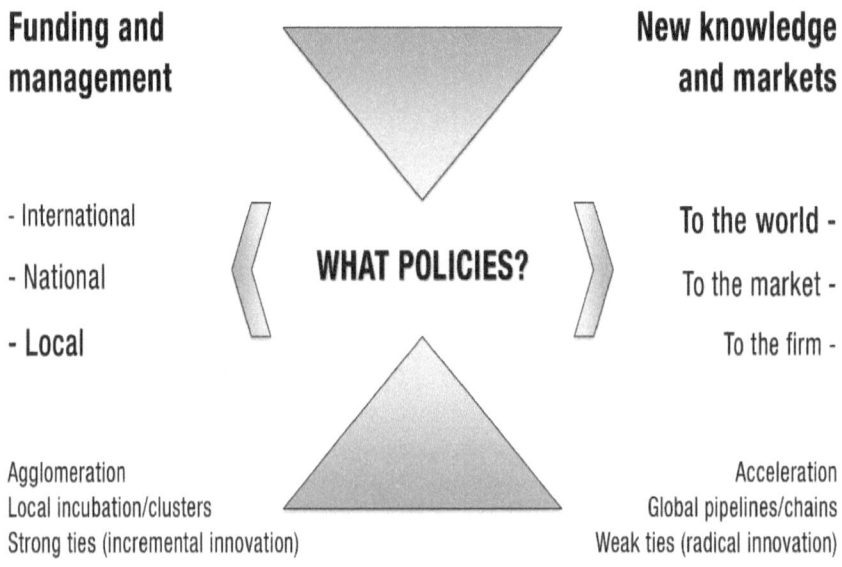

Fig. 1: Tensions between local and global policy management for innovation and competition (Leceta and Konnola, 2016). Source "Unleashing Innovation and Entrepreneurship in Europe: People, Places and Policies", CEPS, 2017.

MULTILEVEL POLICIES

A key issue regarding policies for innovation is to reconcile the natural tension between local resource allocation and desirable global impact. This is so, because "strong connections" in geographically close environments are key for incremental innovations, while "weak connections" through global links can bring more radical innovations (Fitjar and Rodriguez-Pose, 2011). Let us start our first tour in our little exploratory incursion into other programmes that I managed firsthand before addressing the motivations of technological, transnational alliances and, later, the meaning of entrepreneurship and innovation conveyed by people within ecosystems.

Satellites for Everyone?

Low Earth orbiting satellite constellation initiatives for future personal communications.

At least four transnational consortiums have launched a real battle of proposals based on constellations of mutiple satellites in low orbits for personal mobile telecommunications, including messaging services, radio localization, and assistance.

Since the birth of satellite communications, the ultimate paradigm was imagined as a service directly accessible to the user through handheld phones, similar to current cellular telephones. However, with satellites in geostationary orbit (*Geo*) today, the user terminals employ high gain parabolic antennas, to compensate for the high attenuation associated with the signal path in between the user and the satellite. Apparently fixed in the sky, three *Geo* satellites adequately spaced apart along that orbit are enough to cover most of the planet, with the exception of the polar zones.

In contrast, low-orbit satellites (*Leo*) have primarily been used in scientific applications and Earth observation, but a system of communications satellites in low orbit, located between 750 and 1,250 kilometers altitude, would allow a drastic reduction in the size of the antenna required for the user terminals.

However, the movement relative to the Earth's surface of *Leo* satellites requires user terminals to operate with certain monitoring frequency margins due to the Doppler effect and a fairly high number of satellites are necessary to ensure global coverage. In essence, such constellations of communication satellites would be like inverted cellular telephone networks where the cells fly overhead rather than users moving between the cells around terrestrial ground stations.

For instance, the Iridium system, led by Motorola Satellite Communications Incorporated, would be based on a total of 77 satellites located in 7 polar orbital planes at 756 kilometres altitude. Odyssey, proposed by TRV Incorporated, would include 12 medium-altitude satellites at 10,371 kilometres altitude, located in 3 inclined orbital planes. Aries, from Constellation Communications Incorporated, and Globalstar, from Alcatel Qualcomm Satellite Services Incorporated, include 48 *Leo* satellites each. The spectral bandwidth requirements are quite different, from Aries with just 5 MHz to Odyssey's 220 MHz. Some include interconnections via inter-satellite links (ISL) and others operate such interconnections on the ground.

The economic estimates range from $2.3 billion for Iridium to $292 billion for Aries, and $850 billion for Globalstar. The returns from these investments would be obtained generally by monthly instalments of close to $100 subscription rates and from $1 to $3 per minute call. The price of the terminal would be between $1000 and $3000, depending on the production volumes, assuming that the services could start around 1997.

Although some of these proposals have raised scepticism or even hilarity in certain circles, other agents, such as the International Maritime Satellite Organization (Inmarsat), a leading global provider of mobile satellite communications on sea, air, and land and the European Sapace Agency (ESA), recognise the latent potential market.

However, few decisions can be made until the next World Administrative Conference of Radio Communications (WARC 92) decides which portions of the radio frequency spectrum will be allocated to new services. In this sense, other proposals compete for the 1 to 3 GHz band. For example, in addition to those mentioned above, satellite broadcasting aimed at portable and automotive are included.

We must include political reasons to the previously discussed technical and economic challenges in order to anticipate difficult negotiations, which will begin next February in Malaga. So, while many European countries still do not accept there is a need for specific frequency allocations for Leo satellites, the US Federal Communications Commission (US FCC) certainly supports these proposals.

> If this initiative was successful, the natural attractiveness of satellites as an exponent of high tech as well as proximity to the user would be enhanced since this kind of system would represent the basic dial access in remote or isolated settings as a complement to terrestrial cell networks. In the age of the "mini", the question is "can another laptop fit in the pocket of the general public?"

Fig. 2: Illustration from *El País* accompanying the article, November 13, 1991

More recently, I listened to a great expert at the Spanish *Escuela de Organización Industrial* (EOI Business School), Nestor Guerra, challenging Iridium as a paradigmatic failure case and missed opportunity which the new methodologies for innovation would have allowed to manage much better by developing the demand from the outset. This is the core thesis of *The Lean Startup: How Constant Innovation Creates Radically Successful Businesses* by Eric Ries and Steve Blank but also of MIT scholar Luis Perez-Breva in his book *Innovate: A Manifesto for Action*. It is true that the portfolio of innovation management techniques has changed dramatically since the publication of *La gestión de la tecnología y la innovación en las organizaciones* by my dear professors Antonio Hidalgo, Gonzalo León and Julián Pavón back in 2002.

In the last sentence of my press article is where the key to success can be found for a new offering, namely, how many users could actually afford the device and service charge. In the end only the defence sector could. This approach at boosting innovation in the US would be unfeasible at the European Union level, since ESA and the Commission support R & D for civilian purposes. Specialised innovation agencies at national level on their side, such as the CDTI in Spain or the former TEKES in Finland, link participation in national and European programmes bringing together regional agencies and European organisations at the more practical level.

This fragmentary character of the European innovation policy landscape is frequently cited as a long-standing barrier along with so-called "European paradox", whereby Europe would be excellent in producing new knowledge but not so much in exploiting it, resulting in diverging science vs. innovation performance. Hence, the outstanding difficulty in realising the so-called Lisbon Strategy which aimed at making the Old Continent the world's most competitive knowledge-based area in the world. Ultimately, challenges must be incentivizing and motivating, however. And even then, it has taken years to create a new model within the European Union to foster frontier research (the role of the *European*

Research Council) and innovation breakthroughs (which has been later entrusted to the *European Innovation Council*).

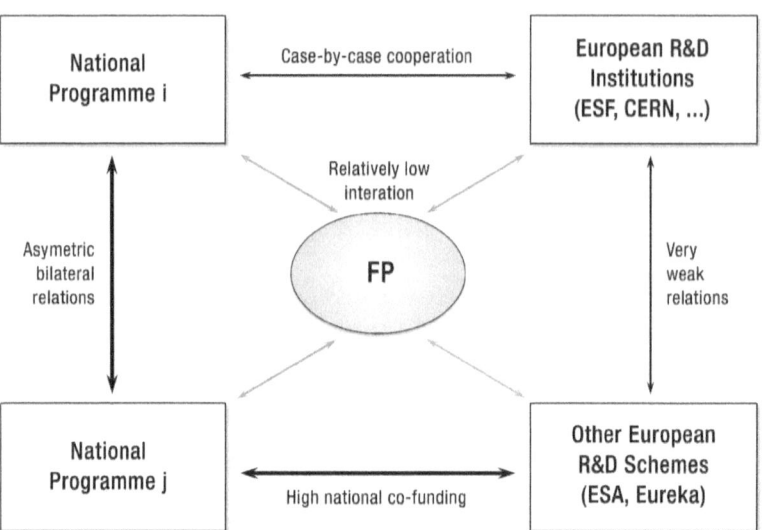

Fig. 3: Conceptual architecture of R&D programmes and organisations in Europe regarding R&D. Source: Prof. Gonzalo León, Technical University of Madrid

Internationalising Regional Strategies

The importance of technological innovation as a driver of competitiveness is one of the most widely established consensus globally. In addition, in the fast-paced race for innovation, it is imperative to develop and access a large knowledge base, which hardly a single company, region, or even a country can accomplish in order to successfully face growing international competition. Also, while creating a favourable environment for innovation is key also in Europe and Spain, open collaboration with partners in other geographical locations provides access not only to new markets but also to new technologies that are not necessarily available within the administrative borders of a single region in Spain or a given State of the European Union (EU).

The empirical evidence gathered during the last decades on so-called "strategic technology alliances" that companies set on their own initiative (without public incentives) show that contract-based consortiums are better and more agile to face the business challenges in technologically dynamic sectors without a need to create new structures or joint ventures that are often expensive, time consuming, and complex. Likewise, technology cooperation may help retain markets and create stable relationships.

Aware of the benefits of joint technological developments by business firms, governments manage cooperation programmes and transnational networks in R&D&I (I+D+i in Spanish) thus promoting excellence and internationalisation of their national innovation systems. This is of interest also to SMEs which have greater difficulties to participate in those programmes and networks due to their size and more limited resources. However, the relative weight of international cooperation in the overall policy mix of most governments and project portfolio of business firms is small. Even in Europe, transnational collaboration in R&D carried out at European level represents just between 15 and 20% of aggregate public spending. On the other hand, public programmes do not always reach all interested parties and knowledge on how to participate is uneven. Therefore, every Member State tries to facilitate access to the EU R&D Framework Programme (EU FP), considering the increasing level of resources available over the years. Consequently, including an international dimension in the overall set of the corresponding strategies, programmes and instruments managed at national and regional governments is critical.

However, balancing local capillarity and global reach is a double challenge for public managers, both nationally and regionally. Through CDTI, the Spanish national innovation agency, the government has been paying increased attention to this since the turn of the century, with a positive commitment also by regional governments and their innovation agencies. Indeed, governments and agencies collaborate jointly to internationalise regional strategies and innovation systems.

Since its foundation around the transition to democracy in the late 70's, CDTI's primary mission was to promote and fund business-led R&D&I projects, both individual and collaborative. Later, since the mid-1980s, CDTI was mandated to promote Spanish participation in international R&D&I programmes in Europe (EU FP, Eureka, ESA, CERN, etc), Ibero-American (Iberoeka) and, more recently since 2005, also with third countries (China, India, Canada, Korea, Japan, etc.) through bilateral programmes managed and financed jointly with counterpart agencies.

With all this, CDTI has become a meeting point for the exchange of good practices among national and regional authorities in the Spanish regions that are committed to foster access to international cooperation programmes where Spain takes part. In each region, counterpart innovation agencies know best the capacities, potential and international experience of constituencies, consequently, harmonising practices and support with CDTI is flexible. Some regions in Spain have incentives and/or dedicated structures as part of their policies and programmes.

In order to foster mutual learning collectively, CDTI organised a first seminar for regional authorities and agencies responsible for innovation at the International University Menéndez Pelayo (UIMP) in Santander, Spain, in 2008. Methodologies were shared in order to draw up specific strategic plans, including targets of participation for each region. To implement and monitor progress with such plans, networks of regional contact points and observatories were decided. This resulted in the creation of a good practices guide that the CDTI issued during its chairmanship of the European Network of Innovation Agencies (TAFTIE) in 2009/2010, gathering all Spanish regional innovation agencies again in Santander in 2009, this time with all national agencies of other European countries present in TAFTIE.

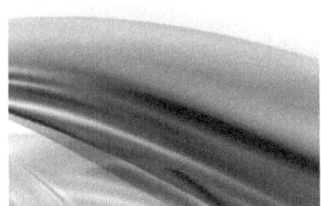

MANUAL DE BUENAS PRÁCTICAS
IDENTIFICADAS EN LAS CC.AA. EN
MATERIA DE APOYO Y PROMOCIÓN
DE LA PARTICIPACIÓN EN PROGRAMAS
INTERNACIONALES DE I+D+i

Fig. 4: Cover of the manual of good practices; outcome of the Summer courses in the UIMP in 2008 and 2009 https://www.cdti.es/recursos/publicaciones/ files / 21316_249249201011027.pdf

Europe As a Technological Opportunity

The Spanish national science-technology-business system received a boost during the first decade of this century with the Spanish government's determination to foster a greater culture of collaboration among all stakeholders through the "INGENIO R&D Plan" led by the Prime Minister's Economic Office. INGENIO included *Consorcios Estratégicos Nacionales de Investigación* Técnica or National Strategic Consortia for Technical Research (CENIT) that were launched and championed by CDTI Director General Maurici Lucena from 2004 to 20210. Paradoxically, considering the growing significance that international analysts and organisations (OECD, 2008) attribute to internationalisation of R&D, the added value of international collaboration in R&D&I for business was unclear. On a more practical level, also, the risk was for crowding out Spanish participation in the EU FP.

Indeed, although in the longer run, more experienced collaborative consortia with CENIT could prepare the basis for an increased participation and leadership in the EU FP context, the challenge for the International Directorate at CDTI was to avoid a national-international substitution effect in the short term. To this end, it was critical to articulate a convincing discourse about the added value for business to participate in international cooperation in innovation related programmes. Following (Narula, 2003), that discourse gravitated around two main ideas. On the one hand, that international collaboration in R&D&I could prepare companies to access global markets with active support of their partners (market access). On the other hand, that international collaboration could enable them to access scientific and technological knowledge that was not necessarily available within the borders of the country or the region of origin (knowledge access).

Clearly, business firms compete in demanding international markets and, to succeed, they need relevant technologies wherever they are. According to the Organization for Economic Co-operation and Development (OECD), around the turn of the century no less than 96.8% of world scientific knowledge and 99.7% of innovation originated outside of Spain. In addition, the increasing complexity of innovation and difficulty of business firms to master all necessary capabilities explain that technological knowledge is increasingly generated via networks.

In this context, the argument at CDTI was that Europe is a unique technology platform for Spanish firms. And the Spanish participation in Eureka, a pan-European network of close-to-market R&D in which Spain has a leading role, gave a good account of their interest. However, als that there was much untapped potential, particularly in relation to the successive editions of the European Union R&D Framework Programme against the risk of Spain becoming a net contributor to the EU budget should we be unable to increase participation and leadership.

Spanish participation in successive EU R&D Framework Programmes had been growing without interruption since the incorporation of Spain to the EU in the mid 80's. In fact, the relative weight of Spanish overall participation in the VI Framework Programme 2003-2006 surpassed that of the relative Spanish weight and contribution to the overall R & D public investment of the European Union. Thus, the evolution of Spanish participation in the R & D community was good, given the degree of development of the national science-technology-business system.

However, while the evolution was positive within the Framework Programme, an imbalance in its composition was detected, characterised by a greater significance and number of projects with Spanish researchers in collaboration with business firms from other European countries rather than the other way around. In short, although Spanish companies had gained more ground on the number of contracts awarded by the European Commission, they did not benefit enough from the flow of technological knowledge available in Europe through the Framework Programme.

The largest business orientation of the VII Framework Programme 2007-2013 illustrated in the launching of *European Technology Platforms* and *Joint Technology Initiatives* (JTI) were opportunities that companies took advantage of. Apart from the significant budget increase of more than 60% on an annual average compared to the previous Framework Programme and the excellent financing (ex. 75% for SMEs), we at CDTI echoed that participating in the VII Framework Programme meant to bet on an excellent R & D, this being a feature characteristic of the EU FP. Also, we stressed that the VII Framework Programme was a sustainable and responsible financing model that we are all funding through Spain's contribution to the community budget.

Therefore, within INGENIO, the Spanish government decided to launch the "EUROINGENIO Action Plan" in 2007 as part of the overall National Strategy for Science and Technology (ENCYT). The strategy precisely identified the strengthening of the international dimension of the National Innovation System as a priority objective of the 2008-2011 Spanish National R&D&I Plan. Likewise, coordination between Ministries was reinforced to create the best *ex ante* conditions in the new initiatives of the European Union with a variable geometry (JTI, PPP, Eranets, etc) in the context of the so-called *European Research Area* (ERA) that was later rebaptised *European Research and Innovation* Area (ERIA).

As a meeting point for go-to-international R&D in Spain, in 2007 the CDTI launched the TECNOEUROPA Incentives Programme, within the EUROINGENIO Action Plan. With almost 9 million euros of subsidies, TECNOEUROPA sought to promote leadership of Spanish companies and incorporate a greater number in the EU R&D FP. To do this, we founded proposal preparation (APC+), technological vouchers for consultancy services and international project offices in national associations and professional colleges. With all this, the CDTI endeavoured to build a strategic relationship with key facilitators and intermediaries, both at the national and regional level, in order to bring European R&D&I closer to beneficiaries.

Progress continued with Horizon 2020 (the EU FP for R&D

in the 2014-2020 period), with a balanced participation against the Spanish contribution to the EU budget. Compared to the former deficit of participation by business, companies tare taking a very active role, convinced now that, through the European Union, they can have access not only of the common European market of goods and services and free movement of capital and people, but also to the most useful technological knowledge for the competitiveness of our economy through strategic alliances with international partners present in the FP. This has continued over the years, resulting in a stable collaborative culture with the best in class, which is very visible also at the aggregate level, Spain being the third largest beneficiary of EU FP and the first one measured by the number of projects led by Spanish entities. Today, one could stress that more and better R&D might also be a way to foster more and better Europe.

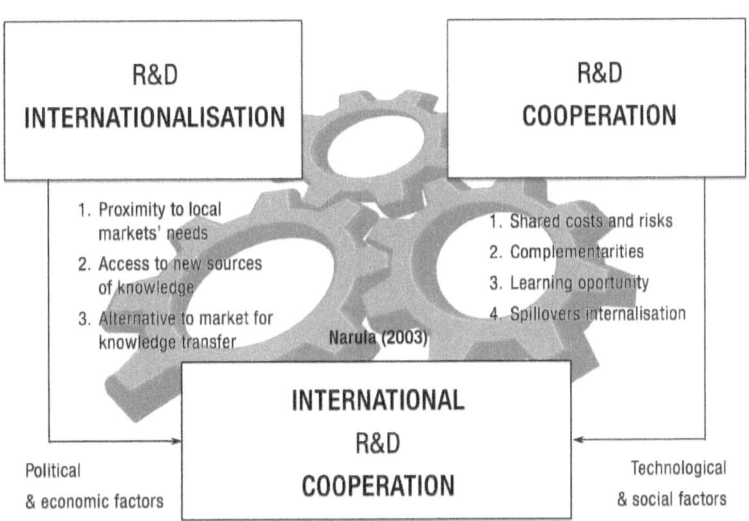

Fig. 5: Explanatory factors of international cooperation in R & D. Source: Narula (2003) and our own elaboration.

JOSE MANUEL LECETA

UNDERLYING DYNAMICS

Innovation with An International Scope

Notwithstanding past achievements with the evolving transformation of the Spanish economy over the last century, there is an emerging consensus on the need to move towards a new model that, in the light of recent developments, appears increasingly urgent. In particular, after the Great Recession that started in 2008 two ideas continue capturing the attention of many business analysts: innovation and internationalisation. And both are closely linked to the extent that some talk about i + i or 'double i', meaning two major levers for Spanish companies to achieve higher levels of competitiveness in a globalised world of business opportunities and challenges. Nevertheless, good intentions will do little good in the absence of the focus and determination necessary to change things for the better on more solid grounds. Let us, therefore, clarify what are the relationships within the "double i" and why it is necessary to go beyond their sum, without confusing desires with realities.

Regarding R&D&I, there is clear evidence since the pioneer work by Robert Solow about the importance of knowledge and the role of business in innovation. Creating favourable conditions from the public sector is advisable, with direct or indirect policy instruments, that incentivise and leverage private sector commitment as well as to favour new business creation and employment in high-tech. At the same time, one should insist on the advantages that companies can obtain by undertaking at least part of their R&D&I activities with an international scope, beyond the customary understanding and casual relationship from innovation to exports.

Such a relation is easy to understand, to the extent that firms that develop technologies that are often costly and complex will obviously have more reasons to market them, not only in their home country but also globally. In the same way, those companies that export are more exposed to competition from other countries and they will more directly feel the need to innovate and increase their productivity by developing and investing in R&D. Beyond such linear relationships, let's clarify what the so-called "internationalisation of R&D" is about and consists of.

Nothing More Useful Than a Good Theory

A seminal paper by professors Daniele Archibugi and Jonathan Michie already in 1995, proposes a taxonomy about the internationalisation of innovation, a phenomenon that had attracted the attention of researchers and institutions in the last decades (UN, OECD, EU, etc.). This is so, as standard economics assumes that R&D is such a strategic business function that companies would always centralise it in their countries of origin. The said paper distinguishes three components.

First, the international exploitation of nationally-produced innovations, through such ancient forms like trade and export of products with built-in technology and, more recently, of unbundled technology through licences, patents, etc. Secondly, global generation of innovations or creation of technological innovations, on an international basis, carried out by multinational corporations with R & D activities in several countries, either newly created or via acquisition of preexisting laboratories and other technological assets. Finally, international cooperation in science and technology that is typically sponsored by governments and that can, in turn, be split into two categories depending on their respective academic or business leadership.

Internationalisation of science led by academia in undertaken in joint scientific projects or shared research facilities, whether large for so-called 'big science' (CERN for example, whenever there is a need of a critical mass of resources that only a group of States can afford together), or 'small science' that is spread out. Other forms of this same phenomena happens through international exchange of researchers, doctoral students, etc which is also very well anchored in the history of catching up countries. Collaboration led by business, in turn, can be implemented via international technological alliances within JVs (joint ventures) or, in the case of dynamic technological sectors, through co-development agreements and contracts.

Categories	Actors	Ways
International exploitation of nationally produced innovations	Companies and individuals	International exploitation of nationally produced innovations International exploitation of nationally produced innovations
Global generation of innovations	Companies and multinationals	Export of innovative goods. Assignment of licences and patents. Production abroad of innovative goods that are developed internally.
Global technical-scientific collaborations	Universities and research centres	Joint scientific projects. Scientific exchanges, sabbaticals. International flow of students.
	Companies national and multinational	Joint ventures for specific innovative projects. Agreements with the exchange of technical information, equipment, etc.

Table 1: Taxonomy of the internationalisation of R & D. Source: Archibugi and Michie, 1995 cited by Molero (coordinator) *Competencia Global y Cambio Tecnológico: un desafío para la economía española*, 2000.

Recognizing the added value of such collaborations, governments foster international programmes and schemes to share costs and risks while taking advantage of synergies and complementarities between participants. This promotes access to the new knowledge available elsewhere and the most dynamic markets for product development. In this connection, Europe has had two major programmes since the 1980s: Eureka, a pan-European network for close-to-market technology co-developments between partners from at least two member States and the EU R&D FP, which has traditionally be until recently of a more pre-competitive nature.

Programmes	Ultimate goal	Novelty required	Evaluation
7th Framework Programme (generation of projects from top-down, with competitive calls and dates)	Strengthening the scientific-technological base for the competitiveness of European industry.	At least new to the European Union as a whole.	Independent and international panels of experts.
Eureka Network Initiative (bottom-up, calls permanently open)	Support transnational inter-business collaboration in its technological dimension.	At least new to the Consortium of partners / countries in their respective markets.	National agencies of the countries present in each consortium.
National / regional (essentially bottom-up, with more or less open calls)	Promote the competitiveness of participating companies by raising their technological level.	At least new to the participating company(s), including development and capacity building.	National experts and agencies responsible for promoting innovation in each country / region.

Table 2: Current outlook of the supporting schemes in Europe for innovation in their international scope: EU FP, Eureka and national programmes. Source: by author.

Ideally, the Framework Programme should support projects that are a novelty in Europe as a whole, rewarding <u>excellence</u> in international class evaluations carried out by independent experts and promoting collaborations also between competitors with a large presence of public and private research institutions. Eureka pays more attention to the <u>relevance</u> of the project for partners and, by extension, the countries that assess and fund them in a decentralised manner, resulting in a large part of the projects emanating from preexisting business relationships between companies, their customers and suppliers. Therefore, although both involve several countries in projects, conditions of participation are very different. While projects of the EU Framework Programme must be collectively new to the European Union, the Eureka projects are required to have sufficient interest for partners of the consortium.

Looking for Multiplicative Factors

A separate issue is to determine the greater or lesser international scope of the innovations developed nationally. To do this, let´s stress that, although every innovation requires a certain degree of novelty, not all innovations are necessarily international and new to the world. In fact, the Oslo OECD Manual distinguishes between new innovations to the firm, to the sector, and to the world. Therefore, the question is how to ensure that a greater number of innovations has a larger international market impact. Beyond participation in the two European programmes cited above, there is a fundamental difference in their significance. One approach is incremental and the another is a radical one that largely corresponds to what is there and what is lacking in the European and Spanish panorama.

To compensate the "transaction costs" the services provided by administrations and business associations to companies should be strengthened thus helping them innovate and internationalise, collaborate, export or invest. Indeed, those companies already operating in international markets deserve support to continue innovating their business models on an international scale and capture "positive externalities". At the same time, support and preferential attention should be provided as well to create and grow new internationally innovative companies that are "born global", given their potential for employment. Now, how can we articulate both issues for existing and new businesses that undertake innovations on an international scale?

The above is difficult to achieve in the absence of adequate structures and schemes. Moreover, it is naive to think that spontaneous projects may arise from the action of national or regional agencies whose work today is essentially financing the technological demand of companies based on domestic needs and local business opportunities. Generating relevant and excellent projects will be more likely and will have higher guarantees of success with more competitive and best practice schemes, including assessments of international experts able to evaluate new ideas and new projects for the companies, but preferably also for those new to the sector or, better still, new to the world. A task as arduous as this may be, is also necessary.

What Innovation Is and Should Be

As with many other key factors for the future of Western societies, general and growing interest in innovation runs the paradoxical risk of becoming a 'common place' that is not well known. Considering the visible achievements of countries with well-established technological trajectories like the US and Japan, as well as the emergence of new actors such as China or South Korea, there is concern about the future role and place of Europe in the knowledge-based economy. To understand and, more importantly, to practise innovation more broadly, we need to know its nature, sources, and dynamics. In that regard, maybe we could consider both positive innovation (what it is) as well as normative innovation (what it should be).

Regarding its nature, we must insist with Schumpeter that not all inventions or new ideas necessarily lead to innovations, since the latter entails placing a product, process, or service with new or improved features in the marketplace. To this end, companies and entrepreneurs are the central agents of innovation and, while some may arise as a result of scientific and technological advances, in most cases there is not a causal relationship from lab to impact. In fact, companies innovate because they believe there is a business need or an opportunity, and generally begin by reviewing and combining existing knowledge before undertaking new developments.

On the other hand, many companies successfully innovate without R&D and on their own means. Rather, they opt for subcontracting or innovating through learning by using equipment, new designs, the skills of the personal or, in general, new forms of organisation, distribution, sale, etc. In Spain, according to surveys of corporate strategies that the National Statistical Institute (INE), a quarter of the innovative products and nearly half of the innovative processes do not carry out any R&D

If the nature of innovation is important, the source or sources is no less so. These may include different combinations of technological and non technological knowledge to innovate depending on the sector or sectors of each company.

Also, an additional complication for public and private managers is that the development of internationally competitive products today requires an ever-expanding array of capabilities and technologies. Added to this are rising development costs, the dizzying pace of new products appearing and, therefore, the reduction of their life cycles and amortisation time of investments caused by obsolescence of former innovations. One way to face this new context is collaboration with other partners in innovation and practising "open innovation," which is the sharing of assets and knowledge to exploit complementarities and overcome the limitations of each firm, thus accelerating the pace of innovation.

But if collaboration is important, it is also worth examining who the partners of the companies are when innovating. The Community Innovation Survey (CIS) shows that the main partners for companies who practise innovative activities are, in the case of Spain, other business firms. First are their suppliers and customers, then universities and research centres, and, lastly, as might be expected, competitors. Differences between countries in the relative importance of these groups have to do with national distribution of companies in areas of high, mid and low technology. However, the multiplicity of company products resulting from the activity of the same company and inputs that are necessary for technological development may result in a mixed picture, as many companies operate across a number of sectors.

Thus, for example, while Finland has the highest rate of collaboration between competitors, probably because of the weight of the ICT sector and the importance of standards in the successful introduction of innovation in this area, it also participates in open innovation with suppliers and customers. In Spain, the highest percentage of collaboration corresponds to suppliers which is consistent with the structure of our economy, including utilities and services. Thus, highlighting the underlying dynamics of spontaneous collaborations is key to nurturing business relationships between companies in their technological and innovative dimensions.

Intra and Inter-Sectoral Dynamics

One of the most cited papers in the economics of innovation literature, authored by Keith Pavitt in the mid-80s, studies the technological innovative patterns of firms and proposes four categories of business sectors. First, science-based businesses such as aeronautics and pharmaceuticals, characterised by their systematic R&D and close relations with academia. Second, those sectors specialising in machinery and instruments whose innovation is based on its engineering capabilities and frequent interactions with their clients. Third are scale-intensive firms that are moderate innovators (automotive and transportation, for example). Finally, other companies that are dominated by their suppliers and sectors from which they obtain most of their knowledge and technology, including machinery and equipment.

The classification is an instrument of enormous interest to analyse business strategies and public policies more adapted to each business sector, also in historical perspective. Indeed, it is also interesting to compare sectoral patterns cited with the moments postulated by historians and theorists of economic development. Thus, proving that largely each successive paradigm has introduced over the years also new ways of innovating and, by extension, new businesses and ways of doing business resulting in sectors and activities that are not replaced but coexist over time.

Period	Techno-economic paradigm according to Freeman (1987)	Industrial organisation	Typical industries	Categories of companies according to Pavitt (1984)
1770-1830	First mechanisation	Growing importance of small manufacturing companies	Textiles, tableware, machinery	Supplier dominated
1840-1880	Steam and train	Separation between producers of capital and consumer goods	Mechanical engineering, steel and coal	Specialised suppliers
1890-1930	Opportunities associated with scientific discoveries	Appearance of large monopoly companies	Chemicals, electrical machines, engineering	Science-based
1940-1980	Taylorist and Fordist revolutions	Oligopolistic competition for mass consumption	Automobiles, pro-synthetic pipelines, goods of mature consumers	Intensive scale
1990-	Information and communications	Company networks, strong interactions user-producer	Microelectronics, telecommunications, software	Intensive in information

Table 3: Relationship between innovative companies and technological paradigms according to Chris Freeman 1987, cited by Daniele Archibuggi, 2000.

Normative or Positive Innovation?

In order to qualify their innovation strategies, it would be misleading to group companies exclusively by their products. For example, it would make little sense to place a company that produces space suits and space boots in the same category as one that produces textiles and shoes or a company that produces precision chains with a heavy industry. In short, rather than discuss sectors, we must talk about companies that are more or less innovative and, by extension, discuss more or less competitive or non-competitive business sectors in international markets.

Capacity building in high and medium technology is a desirable goal for a country, including the creation of new technology-based business firms which are so important for net job creation. But, at the same time, it is necessary to respond to the needs and dynamics of companies in more mature and service sectors, which are key to current employment. All of which sets up a particularly complex scenario in Europe and Spain, addressing both what innovation is and what it should be. In other words, simultaneously practising normative and positive innovation.

Education and Entrepreneurship

Since the last century, Europe faces the challenge of its ageing population but, equally important, also the ageing of its innovative businesses. According to the Institute for Prospective Technological Studies (IPTS, now part of the Joint Research Centre, the science hub of the European Commission) based in Seville, the relative number of world-leading innovative new firms that were created in the last quarter of the last century is ten times lower in Europe compared to the corresponding population in the US. Paradoxically, the economic history of Europe is full of entrepreneurs which are at the origin of the large business corporations that we know today. Europe was thus a continent of innovators... a century ago.

In the years following World War II to the 70s, and in parallel with the growth of large corporations, public policies were then oriented to supporting science and technology, given the general perception that research could 'work miracles'. This laid the foundation of the current social contract with science and the "technology transfer" via publications and patents as well as the linear model of university-firm R&D model, from the lab to the market. This was the universal approach during the second half of the 20th century, based on economies of scale and scope to produce large production series via "creative accumulation" in large companies.

Since the eighties, however, there was a shift induced in multiple sectors by the new information and communication technologies (ICT), a trend which is observed in the resurgence of small companies (start ups, spin offs, spin outs, spin ins) as new innovative agents in the most developed economies: a surprising come back to the initial view of Joseph A. Schumpeter, characterised by "creative destruction." And an unexpected return from "managerial economics" to "entrepreneurial economics" according to professors Audretsch and Thurik, around the turn of the century.

Creative destruction is a return to the entrepreneur. Unfortunately, this was and continues to be a reality in the US more than in Europe if we think that business founders like Nobel and Siemens in Europe, now in the ICT era got names like Gates and Jobs. This is important as the Kauffman Foundation demonstrated that practically all the net jobs created in the US from 1980–2005 were linked to companies of less than five years old. However, in Europe, even though the relative importance of this phenomenon varies as does the degree of development of national economies and the maturity of their sectors, the identification of large enterprises as key drivers of innovation and internationalisation is still very embedded in the collective subconscious and is also the focus of public policies.

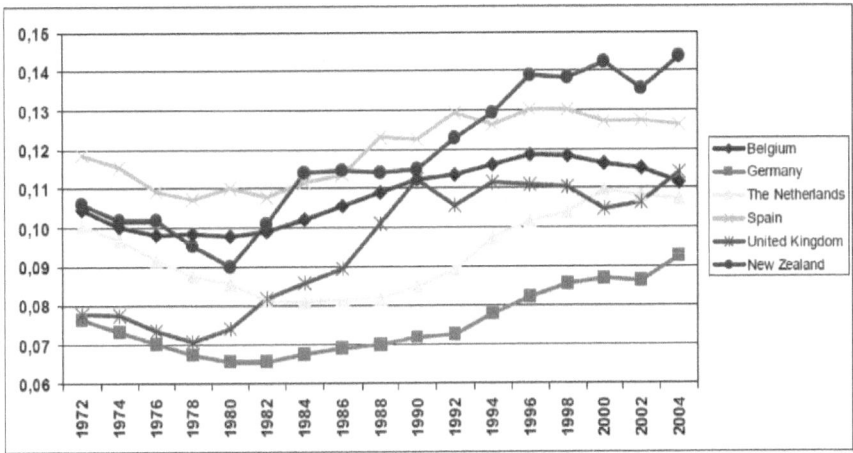

Fig. 6: Business owners to employment ratios in six OECD countries: Van Stel (2005), cited by Thurik (2009), *Enterprenomics: Entrepreneurship, Economic Growth, and Policy.*

New Instruments for New Times

All this has its bearing on the prevailing forms of valorization of knowledge, whose vehicles are essentially three according to the COTEC Foundation in Spain: 1) protection of intellectual property (patents) and its exploitation (licences), 2) collaborative R&D (either via technical assistance, consortia, or sub-contracts), and, last but not least, 3) the creation of new technology-based companies. While the first two are well trodden paths, only since the nineties has the third vehicle received growing attention also in Europe in view of the success of the US in new technology sectors mentioned above, notably microelectronics and software.

	Entrepreneurial Economy	Managerial Economy
Underlying forces	Location Change Employment	Globalisation Continuity Low-wage employment
External environment	Turbulence Diversity Heterogeneity	Stability Specialisation Homogeneity
Operation of the companies	Motivation Market Exchange Competition with cooperation Flexibility	Control Business transactions Competition or cooperation Scale
Public politics	Enable Inputs Local Approach Entrepreneurs	Limit Outputs National focus Established companies

Table 4: Differences between the "entrepreneurial economy" and the "managerial economy" according to Audretsch and Thurik (2004). Source: own elaboration.

In this regard, national and local administrations started investing in new technology-based companies, mainly through the provision of infrastructure and incubation services to favour their creation in early stages such as science and technology parks linked to universities and, to a lesser extent, public agencies for investigation and business parks. Also, with funding in preferential conditions of their business plans to facilitate their consolidation and survival prospects.

According to William J. Baumol in 2004, ICT and biotechnology entrepreneurship particularly in the US advocated that the new firms are the "vehicle" of many breakthrough, new-to-the-world innovations. In fact, more recent studies show that a large part the gap between Europe and the United States in innovation is largely explained by missing startups ("missing yollies" according to Bruegel think tank's researcher, Reinhilde Veugelers, in 2009), whose success requires not just tangible assets and financial resources but also tacit knowledge and skillful teams. Thus, the entrepreneurial economy places the personal element to the foreground, logically coupled with more favourable local or boundary ecosystems to make possible the radical or disruptive entrepreneurial innovation.

SHARE OF *LEADING INNOVATORS* BY AGE COHORT

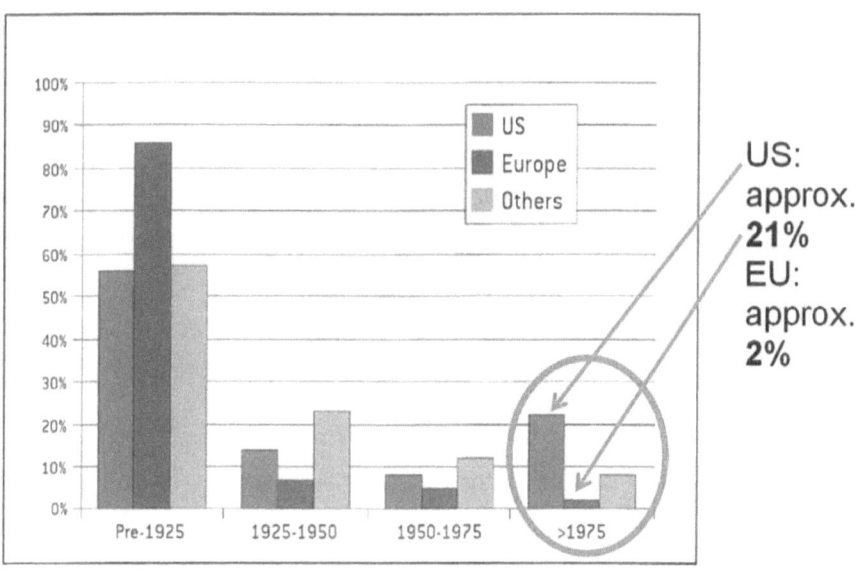

Fig. 7: Age distribution of innovative companies in Europe, the USA, and other countries. Veugelers (2009), published as a "Breughel Policy Brief", March 2009.

Beyond disciplinary knowledge, where the educational system is centered still today, a burning question is how to promote the skills and willingness necessary for future entrepreneurs. On the one hand, there may be intrinsic difficulties since innovation is linked to the agglomeration of local knowledge and capabilities. On the other hand, competition is global, which means further challenges but also opportunities. In that connection, Europe could aim at making the most of its diversity and accelerate world-class innovations but, still today, incubation of new technology-based companies is essentially done on a national basis and there is little support for the acceleration of such companies at the European level.

A notable exception is the European Institute of Innovation and Technology (EIT), which aims to educate the next generation of entrepreneurs through large strategic partnerships called Knowledge and Innovation Communities (KIC). These are formed by partners that make up and integrate the so-called *triangle of knowledge*, of education, research, and innovation. Launched in 2008 with three first KICs in 2010, the EIT is a relatively novel approach that emerged from the evidence that something was missing in the European innovation landscape particularly to mobilise university entrepreneurship, since subsidising science in research centers and financing innovation in existing companies is not enough.

But breakthrough innovations through entrepreneurship requires both talent and determination. Through its KICs, the EIT aims to become a catalyst for change in the way Europe approaches innovation, placing an emphasis on people, particularly young talented people. The following pages are dedicated to this policy experiment, reflecting on its meaning compared to former European policies and programmes.

A FIRST DISCOVERY: Innovation is About People

In July 2011, I assumed the Director position at the EIT HQ in Budapest, Hungary. At that time, innovative entrepreneurship seemed to be a pending debate in Europe which, ten years later, is now almost a commonplace, fortunately.

In Spain for example, everybody talks about entrepreneurship, even at the risk of confusing it with self-employment. But there is no doubt of its social and economic importance, since much of the disruptive innovations that are capable of creating new markets correspond precisely to newly created companies which are, in turn, responsible for the net job creation in the US and the UK, as indicated above.

Ultimately, the challenge and opportunity for the EIT was to respond to the question: why Europe, having excellent research centers, universities, large big business, and a vibrant SME parks, has only managed to create just 2% of the leading global innovators over the last 25 years of the twentieth century, compared with 21% in the US. I then thought to myself that the EIT crystallised a European will to address innovation in a radically different way by focusing on people.

Until recently, science and innovation have come to be understood as the natural division of labour between academia and business, with collaboration in R & D limited to institutional projects where each partner is affiliated and interacts in progress meetings. It is interesting that the European Research Council (ERC), another leading initiative of the "Europe of knowledge" is oriented (like the EIT) towards people, the youth in particular, because the future belongs to them.

On the other hand, entrepreneurial innovation emerge bottom-up, through new business models and value propositions shaped by teams. In addition, the next generation of innovations will clearly go beyond disciplines and geography. Of course, it is necessary to gather the necessary knowledge and skills, but equally important in my view is to nurture attitudes. As discussed above, a 'return to the future' with Joseph A. Schumpeter and his "creative destruction," after a century dominated by the paradigm of large companies and economies of scale.

For all that, the EIT preached everything except 'more of the same' convinced that it would be difficult to obtain different results with 'business as usual'. We believed that, already with its first KICs, the EIT aimed at a radically new approach to stimulate innovation. In those early days in Budapest we used to call KICs our "innovation factories" and the EIT an "impact investment institute" in the view of the founding Board or an "innovation policy lab" in my own opinion.

Indeed, KICs are living partnerships that make up the knowledge triangle, formed by researchers and companies as well as universities and business schools committed to training not only future employees and teachers, but also future employers and leaders. The first results were already visible at the end of 2013 with more than 1,000 students, 100 new companies, and an equivalent number of products that prove entrepreneurship and innovation is possible in Europe.

To this end, the first three communities that were set in motion in 2010 (initially named KIC InnoEnergy, Climate KIC, and EIT ICT Labs). Each had six workplaces that were interconnected across borders to accelerate the growth of new businesses created by students, exposing their business plans to multiple markets and, in many cases, having their first client among large companies part of the KIC to quickly scale their impact and international presence. Its governance is also very original. It is inspired by a business logic where each community is headed by a CEO whose performance is measured by results and impact. It is end-to-end support, demolishing the silos and 'windows mindset'.

The EIT believes that people are the key to the practical exploitation of knowledge. With the launch of up to five more KICs till 2020, and some others potentially later, Europe would have a pan-European ecosystem made up of more than 50 networked centres that stimulate and accelerate 'talent in action' across borders. The European Parliament and the Council assigned 2.7 billion euros to the EIT for the 2014-2020 period, which was nine times more than in the initial 0.3 billions budget. This was a demonstration of confidence by European Union institutions in the EIT, a young and dynamic institute committed to putting our continent back on the path of world-class innovative entrepreneurship.

Certainly, if something positive has come from the decade-long crisis, the Great Recession, it has been a catalytic call to both institutions as well as to the population more generally to conceive new ways of doing things. In a word, *Reinventarse* as the popular Spanish book and author Mario Puig Alonso advocates. From my experience at the EIT between 2011 and 2015, I was able to visibly witness an emerging mobilisation of innovative entrepreneurship in Europe led by people who wanted to take the future in their own hands and improve things.

It was incredibly exciting for me to see the mission of the EIT embodied in the first students of the education programmes of the said three KICs during its first summit in Budapest in November 2013. A community that continues to gather every year by all former and new KICs under the motto INNOVEIT!

PART II.
KNOWLEDGE IN ACTION: LEARNING THROUGH THE PRACTICE OF EIT

NB Sierpinski Triangle. Starting with an equilateral triangle that is divided into four equal triangles and eliminating the central triangle. The same is done with the three remaining triangles and this continues infinitely. It was described in 1915 by Wacław Franciszek Sierpiński (1882-1969), a Polish mathematician with notable contributions for set theory, number theory, topology, and function theory. Two other fractals bear his name in addition to the triangle: the shadow and the curve.

Formally, the mission of the European Institute of Innovation and Technology (EIT) is to promote sustainable European growth and competitiveness and to reinforce the innovative capacity of the member States of the EU to ultimately create the entrepreneurs and innovators of tomorrow. To this end, the EIT sets up strategic partnerships of excellent partners in order to drive innovation from idea to product, from laboratory to market, and from student to entrepreneur.

The EIT fulfils its mission by integrating the knowledge triangle composed of higher education, research and business in Knowledge and Innovation Communities (KIC). By gathering excellent and diverse partners in the KICs, the EIT represents a new agenda for innovation in the European Union, particularly with regard to the mobilisation of higher education institutions.

After a competitive process launched in April 2009, the three first KICs were launched in 2010. These are KIC InnoEnergy (renamed EIT Innoenergy later on) focused on sustainable energy Climate-KIC (EIT Climate KIC) focused on climate change mitigation and adaptation and EIT ICT Labs (EIT Digital) focused on information and communication technologies.

Although the headquarters of the institute is in Budapest, Hungary, the EIT is not concentrated in a centralised campus like traditional institutes, but rather operates in a decentralised and distributed manner throughout its KICs. In turn, each KIC structures its activities around five or six work centres or *co-locations centres* (CLCs). The first three KICs started their operational activities with 17 centres spread across Europe. In addition, Climate-KIC also had other regional application and demonstration centres (RICs) located in six European regions.

The KICs perform a series of activities that cover the complete innovation chain. Likewise, the KICs governance was designed in such a way that allows them to react effectively and flexibly to new challenges and changing environments. To this end, each KIC is constituted as a legal entity and appoints a Chief Executive Officer (CEO) to carry out its operations, which is a novelty in an EU-level initiative. In all, the EIT's KICs are endowed with a high degree of autonomy to define their legal form, internal organisation and working methods.

Essential Characteristics of KICs and Their Partners

The EIT's Knowledge and Innovation Communities (KICs) pursue excellence and relevance in their activities and are established with the final objective of reaching the critical mass necessary to have a systemic impact. They achieve this with the creation of new business, new jobs, new skills and the promotion of talent. Also, KICs are permanently open to new partners, whenever they add value.

Two general concepts can serve to emphasise the creative approach of the Institute's KIC model conceived by the EIT founding Governing Board: a *business logic* in every KIC and an *investment logic* in the relation of the EIT with KICs.

A *business logic* of KICs means:

- High level of integration: each KIC is set up as an independent legal entity, which brings together world partners from the knowledge triangle and establishes a contractual relationship with the EIT.

- Long-term strategic focus: each KIC is configured for a minimum of 7 years so that it eventually becomes *self-sustaining* in the long term after 15 years.

- Sufficient autonomy and flexibility to determine the organisational structure and activities governed by the corresponding KIC Supervisory Board.

- Effective management led by a CEO and a compact team.

And an EIT-KIC *investment logic* means:

- Smart finance and high commitment of the partners: each KIC presents an annual business plan to the EIT whose funding goes up 25% from its total budget over time, and 75% funding from other sources, both public and private.

- Co-location model: each KIC has 5 to 6 access points or *hot spots* of world class innovation benefiting from existing capabilities on the ground.

- Results and activities orientation to impact: the KICs implement a business plan with measurable results and outputs monitored by the EIT.

- Culture: the KICs are formed with a strong entrepreneurial culture.

A Dynamic Partnership Approach: EIT – KICs – Partners

The KICs apply an open strategy regarding new partners. This represents an unprecedented dynamism for a European Union scheme. Specifically, any potential partner can contact the corresponding KIC to express its interest to participate. And the decision is made by the KIC's legal entity and not the EIT.

In addition, the financing model of the EIT is based on the concept of leverage. Each euro invested by the EU budget drags investments from other sources, both public and private, contributing to aligning policy agendas in a flexible and voluntary way from the bottom-up. For 2008-2013, the EIT received precisely €308.7 million from the EU budget to pilot and structure its first operations.

The financial contribution of the EIT is decided every year after evaluation of past performance and business plans of each KIC. Since 2013, a system of competitive reviews was introduced, including the evaluation of results and the economic and financial viability as well as the ambition of the corresponding plans.

Distinct Educational Offer

As already indicated, one of the values of the EIT being added to the European innovation policy scene concerns education, notwithstanding that education is not a EU-level competence. Also, the EIT supports new business creation by the entrepreneurs of tomorrow to promote a practical change in mindset, culture, and attitude. By investing in the EIT, Europe is investing in the talent that might create new companies, as well as to contribute to the ongoing renewal of existing firms.

To that aim, the KICs have developed educational programmes for entrepreneurship and innovation. Specifically, higher education institutions and business in the KICs together offer students the knowledge and skills to be successful entrepreneurs and innovators. Likewise, universities, companies, and research centres collaborate closely with these programmes by offering dual degrees, international and intersectoral mobility, as well as innovation internships in the real business world.

Consequently, the hallmark of the educational programmes of the EIT is not only to teach students to simply access the knowledge but also what to do and how to solve problems with an entrepreneurial mindset, particularly societal challenges. The EIT master's and doctoral programmes train students to be creative, innovative and entrepreneurial. To this end, the EIT has designed specific quality criteria.

Preparing the Entrepreneurs of the Future

Creating more businesses and more jobs through fast-growing, innovative companies is essential for the European Union. Through its KICs, the EIT supports innovation in existing businesses and creates new business opportunities. They are aware that two vital ingredients for the development and growth of new businesses are working within an appropriate context and business skills.

Also, driving a change in perception and recognition of entrepreneurs in Europe is another goal for the EIT. To address and narrow this in the European mindset, EIT creates enabling spaces through its KICs and their CLCs where talent, entrepreneurship and innovation can flourish. Since 2013, the EIT gathers success stories to demonstrate that it is possible to create the conditions, skills, and ecosystems that make possible the change that an entrepreneurial Europe requires.

Through its entrepreneurship programmes, the first three KICs of the EIT launched a range of support services to help candidates translate their ideas into successful businesses. These services focus on various areas such as technology support, market assessment, access to human resources, mentoring advice, seed capital, and venture capital through specific investment funds that KICs are putting in place.

The unique feature of the KIC is to help entrepreneurs from one country access other countries through the network of co-locations and contacts, developing a clear strategy of market penetration, breaking existing national fragmentation, and overcoming the fear of thinking about Europe at an early stage. In each of the respective fields of action of the first three KICs, innovation and entrepreneurship are essential vectors to overcome grand societal challenges. Through its KICs, the EIT aims to develop the next generation of young entrepreneurs, encourage and support people and businesses to develop innovative ideas and bring them to the market, thus contributing to a more dynamic and competitive Europe.

To conclude, I would like to indicate the characteristics that describe what the EIT and its KICs are about, emphasising the distinctive change that the Institute proposed to embody compared to previous innovation support policies in the European Union. To do this, I will point out the suggestions I made during my mandate at the EIT. Perhaps it will be more eloquent to describe what the EIT is by emphasising also what it is not about, starting with its mission statement concerning the people to the government of the institute itself.

- In general, it is about "believing in the talent and courage of people" and, therefore, it is not so much about educating employees but educating employers. It is not about speaking in institutional terms, but how to move forward with concrete cases. Not only with collaboration in R & D, but also with the practical integration of knowledge.

- The governance of the EIT represents an agenda for the European Union as a game changer. It is not about telling you what to do but learning by doing. It is not a linear approximation but a holistic end-to-end service network and it is not programmed top down agenda, but rather bottom up.

- EIT-KICs are living partnerships for co-creation, not just co-financing projects but catalysing strategic alliances. Not research grants but seed investments. The EIT does not consider annual work programmes used in other EU programmes, but annual business plans co-created by KICs.

- KICs are dynamic, end-to-end value generators. As a result, they not only incorporate explicit knowledge, but tacit knowledge as well. They are not closed ecosystems but managed ecosystems. They are not oriented to input or capacity building, but rather to results and impact.

In short, I believe that the way in which the EIT was conceptualised represents a policy innovation for Europe. Nevertheless, 10 years after its foundation, the Institute remains a long-term bet and, therefore, its final impact can only be determined and measured over time. However, it is interesting to reflect on the issues addressed by the first three KICs insofar as they have anticipated emerging trends and new innovation models that have also emerged in Spain more recently.

Reflecting with Historical Imagination

The first time I heard the term *historical imagination* was from Johan Schot, then Director of the SPRU (Science Policy Research Unit at the University of Sussex in the United Kingdom), the first paradigmatic centre focused on innovation studies, set up by its founding Director, Chris Freeman. Johan invited me to present the model of the EIT in 2014. In February 2015, while I was myself a visiting fellow at the Robert Schuman Center for Advanced Studies, we jointly organised a seminar at the European University Institute (EUI) in Florence, Italy, with the pioneer title *Transforming Innovation Policy for Europe*. Thereafter, the term historical imagination found its place in the speech by Johan in London later that year upon receiving the Leonardo Da Vinci medal for his contribution to the history of technology.

Interestingly, from there on, SPRU's focus shifted precisely to transforming innovation policies for a second global transition, as Johan referred to, not that far away from Mariana Mazzucato's mission economy. The emphasis in transition systems is not casual because it is a framework that Johan had developed with Professor Frank W. Geels at MIORI (Manchester Institute of Innovation Research). With this, they both insist that all innovation requires the combination of an idea and its acceptance. Ultimately, the changes are sociotechnical.

In the same vein, in her famous book, *Technological Revolutions and Financial Capital*, Carlota Perez, wife of the previously mentioned founder of SPRU Chris Freeman, addresses the historical analysis of five technological revolutions. These are somehow aligned also with the more recent thesis of the Third Industrial Revolution in Jeremy Rifkin's *Industrial Industry* in 2011 or the Industry 4.0 focused on by Davos in the event organised annually by the World Economic Forum.

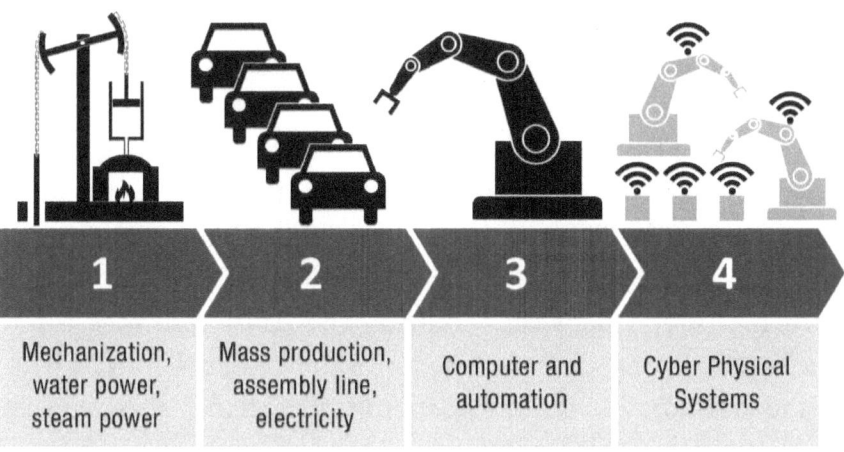

Fig. 8: The phases of Industry 4.0. Source Christoph Roser, All About-Lean. com.

It is stimulating that the issues addressed by the first three KICs of the EIT resemble precisely such historical phases. But few people know that the themes of the first KICs were decided during the German presidency of the EU due to the difficulties to get the EIT off the ground, notwithstanding the personal role by the then President of the European Commission, José Manuel Durao Barroso. The Institute was endowed with an undeniable mission to address energy and climate change. Digital was added, as this is an area where Europe had not found its place despite the fact that digital was a target for Eureca and the EU R&D FP already in the 1980s. Let´s review the historical evolution of what is understood today by Industry 4.0, reflecting on the mission and context of each of the first three KICs .

Climate-KIC: Reinventing Innovation, China

While the world is witnessing the unstoppable emergence of China as a commercial and technological power, modern economic history can hopefully allow us to get inspiration to identify potential future patterns. According to the prestigious scientific journal *Nature,* China already surpassed Europe in 2012 in R&D investment over gross domestic product. And it is overwhelming to think that China could achieve in just a few decades what the West took a century and a half to achieve. In fact, it is worth pondering why the Industrial Revolution took place in Europe between the 18th and 20th centuries (more specifically, in the United Kingdom) and not in China, which, in the opinion of various economic historians, also had the same favourable conditions as the United Kingdom. Such is the thesis of Professor Joseph Needham, who relies on two factors explaining European success and Chinese failure at the dawn of the Industrial Revolution.

On the one hand, China chose to perpetuate a system of innovation based solely on experience, contrary to what happened in Europe where, thanks to the scientific revolution that began in the seventeenth century, a research system was created based on systematic experimentation which allowed to drastically increase the rate of technological innovations. Moreover, the Chinese sociopolitical system at the time did not encourage critical thinking, which is a vital propeller of progress.

Indeed, in nineteenth century China, the ultimate professional ambition was to socially progress in public administration. And the selection system required candidates to learn by heart the Confucius texts, which required a tremendous effort. Needham suggests that, while the Industrial Revolution was taking place in Europe, the brightest minds in China were not dedicated to research and innovation, thus depriving the country of the precious human capital that could have been applied to more productive activities for that economy.

It seems that China today will not repeat those same mistakes. This is one more reason why Europe needs to promote innovation with fresh new policies and determination. *Horizon 2020* and *Horizon Europe* are Europe's big bets on R & D, in which the European Institute of Innovation and Technology (EIT) is embedded. Through its Knowledge and Innovation Communities (KIC), the EIT aims to create a pan-European ecosystem, integrating innovation with the knowledge triangle of business, research institutes, and higher education institutions.

One of these communities focuses precisely on training a new generation of entrepreneurs in the search for solutions to adapt and mitigate the effects of climate change, which is one of the main global social challenges of our time. With hundreds of excellent partners, Climate-KIC (later renamed EIT Climate KIC) is the largest initiative in the European Union for climate innovation, which also involves the participation of (and here is the novelty) municipalities and regions also that add a European dimension to their local operations through this KIC.

In late 2013, Climate-KIC established a major deal in China proposing a low carbon city in Tianjin promoted by the government. Tianjin is the fourth largest municipality in the country. Chinese cities are at the front line facing the challenges of climate change, sustainable development, and demographic change, making it a testing ground of great interest. In this connection, the evolution of the city model in China in the coming decades is also crucial for the rest of the world.

Also in Europe, Climate-KIC has several regional centres (RICs) where municipalities incorporate and test green buildings and smart energy management systems, mobility, and so on. In fact, 60 to 80% of global actions to reduce greenhouse gas emissions takes place at a subnational level. A strategic objective of the RICs network was to influence the allocation of 325,000 million euros from the Structural Funds of the European Union for the 2014-2020 period through pilot projects, innovative public procurement, educational programmes for professional competencies, intersectoral mentoring, training for entrepreneurship, etc.

Climate-KIC is also present in Spain with a regional centre in Valencia, where a major event for Climate-KIC innovation took place in the autumn of 2014. Beyond having a dynamic and entrepreneurial spirit that is above the Spanish average, Valencia region is committed to include the EIT in their strategic plans with an emphasis on ecosystems and talent, because innovation is a local phenomenon whose impact can overwhelm geographical, disciplinary, and sectoral boundaries. It is high time to give a voice to entrepreneurs and to reinvent innovation.

KIC InnoEnergy: Innovative Value Chains, Europe.

Historian Daniel Yergin in *The Quest: Energy, Security and the Remaking of the Modern World* recalls that, in the middle of the 19th century, Lord Kelvin himself warned about the dependence on coal to support the industrial development of the United Kingdom since, in only two centuries, consumption had doubled per capita. A development made possible by the availability of an immense amount of cheap and easy to use concentrated energy thanks to the extensive use of fossil fuels. The use of coal, followed by oil and gas, marked a time of heat and movement that would result in the name given to energy science: thermodynamics. Later on with electrification, Europe would show the world its faith in progress at the Universal Exhibition in Paris in 1900 with its famous Palace of Electricity.

But also around 1914, more than a century ago, many new technologies were created for military use during the Great War. This was due to the instability in Eastern Europe, causing the Old Continent to reorient its energy policy. In recent publications, the Bruegel think tank from Brussels ponders how we can replace our external dependence on Russian gas and integrate the internal electricity market in the EU. A challenging opportunity for Europe to innovate the entire value chain from generation to consumption as well as new primary energy sources coupled with greater end-to-end efficiency. These are very relevant objectives if we recall that, on average, 27% of the cost of the goods we consume is energy.

Fig. 9: The Palace of Electricity at night at the Universal Exhibition of Paris in 1900. It was as emblematic as the Eiffel Tower was in the previous exhibition of 1889.

In the energy field, the European Institute of Innovation and Technology (EIT) has another focus with the KIC InnoEnergy (later renamed EIT InnoEnergy). KIC InnoEnergy is one of the Knowledge and Innovation Communities of the first wave launched in 2010 by the EIT. Formally, KIC InnoEnergy is a European company made up of universities, research centres, and business firms with the ambition of becoming the European engine of entrepreneurship and innovation in sustainable energy. With innovation hot spots in six EU regions, KIC InnoEnergy's support is a continuum, from educating future energy leaders in order to accelerate world-class startups through products and services that reduce the final cost of energy, increase the security of supply, or reduce greenhouse gas emissions.

Business leaders, such as Natural Gas, Total, and EDF or ABB decided to participate in KIC InnoEnergy, whose transnational nature is a paradigmatic example of open innovation in global networks (OECD 2008). Notwithstanding their established leadership positions, these large corporations need to strengthen the efficiency of their businesses against international competition and incorporate new added value services to create new potential growth paths in the future. Thus, intra- entrepreneurship and entrepreneurship can work hand in hand.

As already mentioned before, according to data from the innovation community survey, the main partners of innovative businesses are other companies. They are suppliers and customers first, then universities and research centres and, finally, competitors. In this context, Spanish multinationals, particularly infrastructure operators and service providers, can work towards innovation by reinventing their value chains to make their partners innovate and attract future game changers.

KIC InnoEnergy's postgraduate educational programme attracted more than 5,000 students from all over the world until 2013, of which close to 400 were selected and awarded scholarships thanks to the EIT grant. Five of the 100 graduates outperformed all leading universities in the world in the 2012 *Clinton Hult Global Challenge*. The number of non-European candidates and participants is also striking with over 80% of students in the first editions and 50% in later ones.

It is thus fortunate that KIC InnoEnergy established a centre in Barcelona at its outset and, although Spain did not participate that intensively in the first Industrial Revolution, it is now managing the use of wind to produce electricity, which is cost comparable to coal or gas. However, no one has a monopoly on talent. Attracting and retaining it is the long-term key because, as Daniel Yergin noted in the already cited work, "Energy solutions of the XXI century will be on the minds of people around the world and this resource base is growing."

EIT ICT Labs: Disruptive Collaboration, USA.

One of the fathers of computer science, the Hungarian-American John von Neumann, exemplifies in his transatlantic biography that the transition of technological leadership from the Old to the New Continent has been exacerbated in recent decades with the information revolution. In his posthumous book, *The Computer and the Brain* (translated into Spanish by a young Josep Borrell in the 1980s), von Neumann reflects on the links and differences between the functioning of the two. Von Neumann's computer architecture was revolutionary as he proposed that the computer will store its own instructions in its memory, which is a giant step in making these new machines reprogrammable. Von Neumann thought that the main job of the computer would be one in which the machine serves as an experiment simulator that would otherwise be too costly or impossible to carry out. An idea that today takes on a new meaning in relation to entrepreneurship and collaboration between actors in open innovation ecosystems.

Until recently, the term "new technologies" came to be synonymous with "information and communication technologies" (ICT). The emergence of entrepreneurship has brought stories and personalities alongside electronic gadgets. Some of them are relatively new like Mark Zuckerberg (Facebook), Larry Page and Sergei Brin (Google), and Jeff Bezos (Amazon), while others are veteran icons, such as Steve Jobs (Apple) and Bill Gates (Microsoft), are just as present as the younger icons in the collective imaginary. What fascination do all these people share? Perhaps that innovation, like invention, discovery, creativity and so many other unique powers of the human being, have an aura of mystery and magic. The creation of startups does not cease to be an exploration into the unknown.

An exploration where some leading authors, such as Clayton Christensen or Steve Blank, pioneers respectively of the disruptive innovation theory and the lean startup movement, propose a set of guiding principles for generating new business. Very much as Peter Drucker did with the management of existing business firms, in a special issue published in 2014, the *The Economist* magazine, believes that the new methods for those embarking on the adventure of creating a new company to better manage risks and uncertainty are starting to be spelt out. However, Blank says that startups are not small versions of large companies, simply because the latter run known business models while startups explore new business models, as temporary organisations in the search of a scalable value proposition.

On the other hand, digitisation is already transforming very diverse businesses. Previous disruptions were characterised by quick technological advances and commercial innovations from the laboratory to the market at the time new sectors were being created. Over time, improvements in key technologies slowed and the most important innovations were made in deployment, production at scale, and distribution, as the technologies and their applications became ubiquitous and widely used. Prime examples are in the electricity and automotive industries.

When we talk about ICT, everything is distinct and its impact is unprecedented in history. As John Hagel, co-chairman of the *Center for the Edge Deloitte* points out, "It is the first technology that has demonstrated sustained exponential improvements in price and performance over a long period of time, that will foreseeably continue to grow in the future." This brings to mind *Moore's Law*, postulated for semiconductor devices with a very rapid growth rate in terms of capacity and processing speed. This is precisely what underpins the development of ICTs. This vertigo also affects business models that are becoming obsolete, as evidenced in the renewal of large companies in international rankings like Forbes.

Moreover, disruptive innovation, not to be confused with radical innovation that relates to the development and not the adoption of technologies, has been democratised largely by the introduction of ICT to other sectors and everyday uses. From booking a taxi to digitising former monopolies from the inside, such as telecommunication and its traditional connectivity business. The phenomenon of *FinTech* shows revealing cases with the association between new technology start ups and banking as well as statements made by large transport or automobile companies such as Lufthansa or VW that see themselves as software companies in the future. The *incumbents* are already in the process of disruptive innovation.

FRACTAL INNOVATION

Classification of Strategic Innovations	Features According to Price and Demand	Classification of Capacities and Markets	Value Proposition and Associated Dynamics
Sustained Innovation:	Higher unit price. Your clients ask you	Improved competition	Builds upon current performance, continuous improvement, efficiency, 6 sigma, etc. Operational innovation
		Destruction competition	Radical or "breakthrough". Requires a general rethinking
Disruptive Innovation:	Lower unit price. Your customers are NOT asking you	Disruptive same market	They are customers who already consume (something similar or from that industry)
		Disruptive new market	They are customers who do not consume (they did not have access to the necessary capital or knowledge)

Table 5: Strategic innovation according to Professor Juan Pablo Vázquez Sampere, from IE Business School in Barcelona, Spain.

While young innovative companies are key to net employment generation and responsible for a large share of breakthrough, disruptive innovations (Baumol 2004), new businesses creation is a necessary but not sufficient condition. Mariana Mazzucato, for instance, in her book *The Entrepreneurial State* defends the need for public and regulation. The key is also the context in which new firms can scale-up and become effective international leaders over the years.

In a way, such is also the thesis of the World Economic Forum (WEF, 2014 and 2015) that recommends Europe to approach the next wave of entrepreneurship as a three phase cycle consisting of stand up, startup and scale-up and facilitate all this with next generation innovation policies, which are interestingly aligned with the three pillars of activities that the European Institute of Innovation and Technology (EIT) promotes through its Knowledge and Innovation Communities (KICs).

The third of its first wave of KICs that the EIT launched focused precisely on the information society: EIT ICT Labs (later renamed EIT Digital) whose three pillars of activity are comprised, like any other KIC, of education for entrepreneurship (stand up), encourage the creation of new businesses (startup), and support business growth with world-class innovations (scale-up).

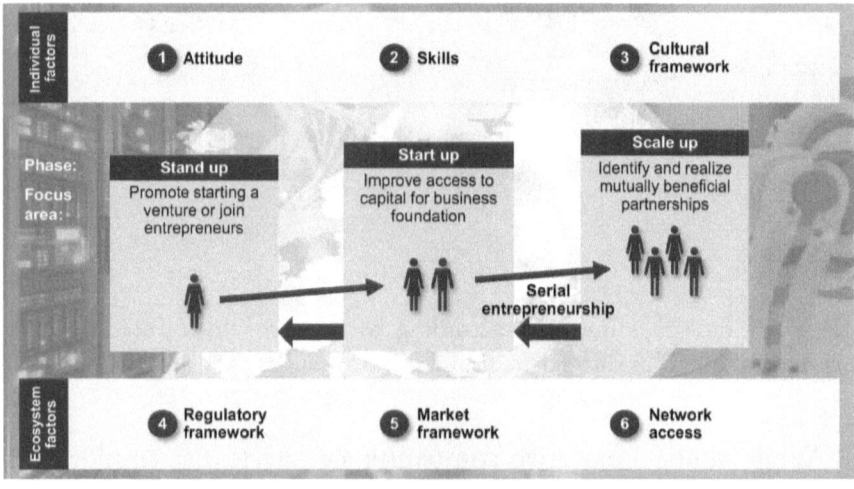

Fig. 10: Proposal of the World Economic Forum for a more innovative and entrepreneurial Europe in its report of June 2014 "Fostering Innovation-Driven Entrepreneurship" in Europe. I also contributed to a follow on report in 2015.[1]

In the search for innovative policies for ICT in Europe, EIT ICT Labs builds upon existing capabilities to align public and private action. Increasingly, there is more and more support for *web entrepreneurs* in Europe, but the KIC is unique not only because of its transnational dimension, but also because of its willingness to provide for an end-to-end, seamless supportive environment or pan-European ecosystem. And since the most promising ideas may come from the periphery, EIT ICT Labs strives to link and scale up entrepreneurial teams together with large telecommunications companies and operators, which Europe does have, as these also need to reinvent themselves and digitise also their connectivity business.

If EIT ICT Labs is part of the answer for Europe to find its place in the future world of ICT by developing a larger group of innovative world-class leaders, it will also depend on Spain since Madrid has a co-location centre connected to the rest of established centres of EIT ICT Labs based in Berlin, Eindhoven, Stockholm, Helsinki, London, Paris, Trento, and Budapest. Supported by partners like Telefónica, Indra, Atos, UPM, IMDEA, and the Barcelona Supercomputing Center (BSC), Spain may also have its say and chance to promote the development of disruptive services and applications. EIT ICT Labs also has an antenna in Silicon Valley through a centre in Palo Alto that has been in operation since 2015.

History can be a source of great inspiration, indeed. With that in mind, let us remember that the pioneering development of global telecommunications is also connected to Spain and Madrid, which hosted the international conference where the specialised agency of the United Nations was created, the International Telecommunication Union (ITU), headquartered in Geneva. This agency unified two former parallel fields of wire telecommunications and radiocommunications. Also the deployment of the *Compañía*

Telefónica Nacional de España was, to a large extent, a transatlantic entrepreneurial adventure that has achieved a significant place in the world thanks to its strategic operations, first in Latin America, then in Europe, and more recently in Asia. But if it is true that history repeats itself, it will always be different, since, as Ortega said, human nature is futuristic and projective.

What Does This Mean for Spain? First Results of the E2I2 Forum of the Spanish Royal Academy of Engineering

In the middle of my term at the EIT, I met with the then President of the Spanish Royal Academy of Engineering and renowned university professor, Aníbal Figueiras, during a congress organised by the Alianza Cuatro Universidades (A4U) at the headquarters of Telefónica.[1] Soon thereafter, Aníbal facilitated a contact also with his successor at the Academy, Elías Fereres, and both were very interested in knowing and disseminating the lessons learned from the EIT across Spain. With this idea in mind, I worked with the hard-working managing director, Javier Pérez de Vargas, to structure a forum that we came to call Education, Entrepreneurship, Innovation, and Investment (E2I2 Forum). The Forum was presented to the public in 2014 as a strategic initiative of the Academy to promote a global reflection on the Spanish innovation system and to help "overcome the traditional separation between science-engineering and innovation in the business sector."

---

1 https://portal.uc3m.es/portal/page/portal/investigacion/parque_cientifico/actualidad_agenda/noticia-a4eu-november-2013 / programa% 205y6% 20nov_impreso.pdf

Ultimately, the initiative aimed to contribute to the better use of the talent that exists in both academia and industry by encouraging a more entrepreneurial thinking and mindset in both. To develop the initiative, the Royal Academy collaborated with associations and organisations such as *Transforma España Foundation*, *RedEmprendia*, and *Insight Foresight Institute*. The initiative was also a sort of pilot inspired by the US National Academies in Washington. My good friend, Charles Wessner, former director for innovation and entrepreneurship at the Academies and now at George Washington University, also supported us.

Regarding the *modus operandi* of the Forum, participants were asked to share their experiences and knowledge of international trends along three pillar domains. These pillars served to structure the reflections from the bottom up and not "silos" since the success of the overall initiative was judged to depend on the whole vision and recommendations for the (eco)system. Three groups were formed for:

- Education (led by *Transforma España Foundation*). Promotion of education for entrepreneurship, not only in relation to students and business incubation, but also in the training provided by university professors and non-university teaching staff.

- Innovation (led by *Insight Foresight Institute*). Promotion of the practice of innovation in large and small companies in their relationship with new (start-ups and spin-offs), analysis of different management models of open innovation and intrapreneurship.

- Entrepreneurship (led by *RedEmprendia*). Promotion of new entrepreneurship models that would allow Spain to improve its structural deficit in medium and high technology sectors, support for the creation of new innovative enterprises and their growth, etc.

Each group had a dual approach of identifying good practices and relevant international trends for Spain and identifying the main problems, needs, and proposals for action in each of the pillars. The presentation of the results took place in mid-2017. And I published three press articles with collaborators of the Forum reproduced hereafter: Senen Barro, Alejandro Tosina and Totti Konnola.

These are found below in the order in which they appeared in the press. Like at the Forum, where former professors like Elias Muñoz Merino and José Antonio Martín Pereda were particularly active, the articles discuss how to transfer to Spain the institutional, governance, management and operational learnings of the EIT against the three areas of education, innovation, and entrepreneurship.

ENTREPRENEURSHIP:
Vitamin D For Our Companies[2]

A deficit of Vitamin D prevents proper regulation of calcium and phosphate levels, which can lead to bone damage and rickets. Probably also the Spanish entrepreneurial ecosystem lacks sufficient Vitamin D, which explains why our companies, particularly technology-based new firms, do not grow as much as they should. This is not just a problem for the company itself but also for the development of present and future productive "tissue", with implications for job creation and wealth. In fact, the small size

---

2 The text corresponds basically to the press article written together with Senen Barro and published in the newspaper El Mundo on 16 January 2016.

of Spanish businesses negatively affects the country's productivity. Indeed, there is empirical evidence showing that the employees of small and medium-sized companies are less productive than those of larger firms. This is evidenced by a study on business demography made by the Spanish *Fundación de Estudios de Economía Aplicada (Fedea)*. According to that study, if the Spanish business community was comparable in size to that of Germany or the UK, our GDP would be 15% higher. Among the causes are the low quality of business management and a less stimulating regulatory framework.

Start-ups and spin-offs play an essential role in this regard. They are companies that generate high-quality employment and a source of innovation for other companies. They energise the productive fabric around them and favour the transfer of knowledge and talent. Spain, which had a chronic lack of these kinds of new innovative businesses, has created an improved breeding ground over the last decade. Nowadays, entrepreneurship is spoken of favourably everywhere as a positive culture, public and private initiatives that support entrepreneurship are multiplying, there is financing for early stages, and there are so many incubators that an entrepreneur could almost live in a parallel business world, going from one to another without setting foot in the market. The problem today is not so much the venture in its early stages, but the difficulties in expansion and internationalisation of these business initiatives. In fact, among the new companies, those that are the most innovative, and are knowledge and technology-based, do not scale up to the extent they do in other countries with more fertile and settled ecosystems.

Curiously, the only European company created since 1975 that is in the world's top 500 is Inditex from Spain. We also have other Spain-born examples of young leading innovative companies with strong growth ("yollies" mentioned before), such as eDreams, Privalia, Scytl, Zed, and Idealist. But we must also face the fact that many other equally promising entrepreneurial initiatives quickly disappear or do not grow as they could. What is the reason for our companies becoming sick with "rickets", particularly those based on knowledge and technology? How can we get the most promising companies to scale-up properly? These are some of the questions that the Education, Entrepreneurship, Innovation, and Investment Forum (Forum E2I2) of the Spanish Royal Academy of Engineering of Spain (RAIng) address in the chapter on "high growth potential companies."

This chapter is coordinated by RedEmprendia, the leading university network in Ibero-America on innovation and entrepreneurship sponsored by the Santander Bank.

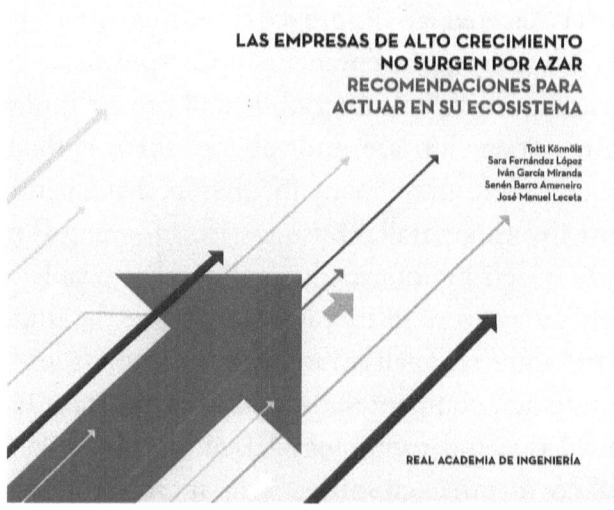

Fig. 11: Cover of the study edited by the Royal Academy of Engineering https://www.raing.es/pdf/publicaciones/libros/las_empresas_de_alto_crecimiento.pdf

For these companies to grow more rapidly and firmly, an enabling environment and acceleration agents are needed, helping them scale and internationalise across Europe and beyond. Funds from angel investors, central government and regional institutions, and seed capital are relatively abundant in Spain in the early stages. However, funds are scarce in more advanced stages of these companies when the investments required are not in the amount of a few dozen or hundreds of thousands of euros but in the millions. In any case, the outlook is improving in this regard too, with a growing number of investment funds, including foreign capital.

Another critical factor for our structural shortcomings in Spain concerns the education on starting up and training for specific business skills well before higher education. Almost all experts agree that an entrepreneur is not born but made, but this actually happens at birth. Educational factors decisively influence not only the vocational aspect of an entrepreneur, especially in terms of attitude, but one's skills as well, which are a fundamental factor for the success of a business. Furthermore, it is not the same type of entrepreneurial talent that is needed to start a business as it is to scale it up. This is where we have a very important handicap.

According to a famous African aphorism, it takes a tribe to educate a child. It is the same for a company to consolidate, grow rapidly. and even reach international markets. A company needs a complete system composed of public administrations, universities, Public Research Organizations (PRO), other companies, and society as a whole to value the role of entrepreneurs and celebrate their cases. This is the recent thesis of the OECD due to the evidence that shows that public policies that are limited to the two extremes (micro and macro) are not enough to promote growth. The meso level and the ecosystem are also key. This holistic vision is pivotal in the study that the E2I2 Forum has commissioned *Insight Foresight Institute (IFI)* to carry out an empirical research to help companies with high innovative potential, including spin-offs and start-ups, grow and internationalise quickly. Our prosperity is at stake and this is why we are dedicating the attention from

RAIng, *RedEmprendia* and IFI. And we are certain that the effort will benefit us all.

INNOVATION: Entrepreneur or Small Businessperson?

Entrepreneurship is fashionable. Concerning the traditional scarcity and modest social assessment of business vocations in Spain, there is a paradoxical impact of the Great Recession. Namely, that society is now embracing the entrepreneurial paradigm as a "mantra" in an effort to support higher hopes for the future.

In fact, entrepreneurship as a function and entrepreneurs themselves as agents of innovation are areas of socio-economic research of growing interest, both in academia and business since Joseph A. Schumpeter postulated his concept of "creative destruction" in the first part of the last century. The contribution that newly created companies provide to economic growth, employment, and breakthrough innovation in an increasingly globalised environment has been highlighted in recent years (Kauffman and NESTA, for instance), thus motivating public and private initiatives to foster an entrepreneurial spirit.

Much of the research in this area has focused mainly on the profile of the entrepreneur as an individual as well as on their strategies for creating new businesses in environments that are favourable at the social and macro level with paradigmatic examples such as Silicon Valley, Israel, and Singapore. Nevertheless, there are also opportunities for entrepreneurship within established organisations and corporations, through intra-entrepreneurship. On the other hand, there is also empirical evidence that shows that modest expectations for growth in an existing market may drive companies to seek disruptive innovations in order to boost that market or create new ones to achieve new business opportunities.

However, the international rankings of leading companies are increasingly volatile and established companies are also aware of the need to transform and change their business models. Clayton Christensen, intellectual heir of Schumpeter, insists on the "dilemma of the innovator" to explain the paradox that a firm can still make mistakes even when doing the right thing, namely, to follow its current customers. This is where a fundamental difference between an entrepreneur and a businessperson lies. Business management is based on an analysis of the data which is only available from the past. The problem arises when managers try to do something that has not been done before or the future becomes very different.

Therefore, it is more difficult to fit creativity, a maverick spirit, and the need for autonomy that characterise an entrepreneur in the canonical field of business plans. Particularly, business models that are settled, with stable processes that have been tested, solid hierarchy and, moreover, in which the corporate culture is rooted and linked to more traditional ways of doing business that inhibits the emergence and retention of unorthodox ideas. Let's also recall that Management Business Administration (MBA) degrees have been awarded for more than a century now.

In addition to the mobilisation of internal talent, the need for cooperation with other actors in the ecosystem (research centres, external entrepreneurs, start-ups, investors, etc.) is becoming an increasingly important strategy for technological intelligence and market, establishing cooperation and co-creation networks with the objective of providing greater value to potential customers and partners. In this regard, the growing activities in the field of *corporate venturing*, through specialised groups in startups created in the margins of, practically, every large corporation, is also a relevant trend. Through accelerators or funds, large corporations seek to access new technologies, disruptive innovation, or new ways of serving customers and they do this within increasingly blurred and convergent sectors.

In this regard, the World Economic Forum (WEF, 2014 and 2015 reports), NESTA and CEPS as well as other opinion leaders are calling attention to the importance and potential of collaborations between established companies and new firms. From the procurement of technologies that characterise the economic convergence phase and collaboration between public-private R & D where most of the public policy lies still today in Europe, we are undoubtedly witnessing a third stage characterised by the exploration of more disruptive forms of innovation through entrepreneurship, venture capital funds, accelerators, etc.

The scenario has changed also in Spain where virtually all large companies have open innovation and intra-entrepreneurship support lines as part of their strategies. Taylor gave way to Schumpeter long ago. However, we are far from a dominating design and there are no patterns tailored to each sector for such strategies. What models are the large Spanish companies using to maintain their market position in the face of new entrants? How have the more consolidated companies managed to mobilise their internal talent and become increasingly agile and disruptive? Is *corporate venturing* a useful tool for the creation of innovative ecosystems within or around large corporations? What barriers for innovation and entrepreneurship do these companies detect when looking for better opportunities?

These are just some of the questions addressed by the Education, Entrepreneurship, Innovation, and Investment Forum (Forum E2I2) of the Royal Academy of Engineering of Spain (RAIng) as part of its reflection regarding current limitations of the innovation (eco) system in Spain. The Forum tries to help overcome these limitations by analysing the most recent international trends and focus on people as agents of change. The Royal Academy of Engineering seeks to become an organ for debate and evaluation, independent of the policies in this area and similar to the mechanism of the US National Academies in Washington. They try to do this with a rigorous but practical understanding of the phenomena of entrepreneurship and innovation in Spain, going beyond clichés and slogans.

In particular, the work stream on corporate innovation, sponsored by the RAIng in collaboration with I*nsight Foresight Institute (IFI)*, focuses on different innovative management models launched by large companies across Spain and identifies good practices to formulate recommendations that would allow them to advance in second- generation designs for corporate ecosystems that are much more efficient and dynamic and tailored to their business. Ultimately, it is all about "innovating innovation", also within corporations because, as Albert Einstein said, we can hardly solve our problems with the same level of thinking that created them.

EDUCATION: A European California

At the time the Spanish Foundation of the Technological Cooperation (Cotec) celebrated its first *Imperdible* event in the Spring of 2016, a symptomatic and terrible image of a giant pyre of burning tires near Seseña was seen on TV. Had there been good regulation at the time, its processing would have turned into a business opportunity as well as a great service to the environment. Since the 70s, MIT professor Nicholas Ashford and more recently, Andrea Renda of the European think tank CEPS, found evidence that suitable regulations can create innovation, particularly to address major societal challenges. On the contrary, bad regulations not only spoil opportunities for innovation, but potential innovators, professionals, and entrepreneurs are inhibited as they do see the need to do things differently.

Fortunately, if institutions are the carriers of history, people are the drivers of the future. For instance, the European Commission sponsored some *innovation deals* based on former experiences by The Netherlands and it was stimulating to see a European Commissioner, the economist Carlos Moedas leading the Directorate General for R&D which has traditionally been dominated by the logic of science. This combination of regulation, appetite for knowledge and risk must be completed with a clear result orientation, because if something good was to come from a Great Recession, it is precisely the invitation for everyone, institutions and individuals, to rethink their work and perhaps go beyond their obligations.

As we know, every innovation is a novelty, but not every novelty is an innovation. In Spain, we adopted the United Kingdom's former model of business innovation and skills within the Ministry of Economic Affairs, but this passage did not actually serve to achieve a new social contract for science and innovation. Our traditional model of R&D&I (I+D+i in Spanish) has been there for too long. No one can say that we have not had the opportunity to reflect on the goals unachieved and how to correct the course of action. Oscar Wilde said it best, "there is no such thing as a moral or an immoral book. Books are well written or badly written."

This is a challenge for our time and generation. During the Cotec event, King Felipe VI said that if Spain had managed to place itself in the world elite in sports, nothing prevented us from doing so in innovation. That is true. Imagine Spain as the California of southern Europe. A place where people not only think about retiring but where they want to live and work. The sun and the beaches can attract active talent committed to generating wealth, social progress, and respect for the environment. There is no objective reason that prevents this vision from being realised nor Germans, for example, have reasons to live structurally better than Spaniards.

On the contrary, those of us who have lived far away think like Javier Mariscal[3] when he confessed in an interview published in *El País* on November 4, 2015, while walking along the *Paseo del Prado* from the Atocha railway station in Madrid: "The light that bathes Spain is a song to life." Innovation, like life, is a journey, as the former director of Telefónica I + D, Carlos Domingo would say. Citizens still believe that the most important public spending is on health and education. They may be right that these are good policies also for science and innovation in the long run because, ultimately, it is all about the talent of three generations in order to make up the texture of any historical moment, as Ortega would argue.

We must therefore welcome a debate on education that also addresses education for innovation and entrepreneurship, as proposed by the Royal Academy of Engineering in the E2I2 Forum (Education, Entrepreneurship, Innovation, and Investment) because the relationship between research and innovation is much more established than the relationship between education and entrepreneurship in policies. Inspired by recent international trends towards the integration of the knowledge triangle, the vision of the E2I2 Forum matches the European

---

3 https://elpais.com/cultura/2015/11/03/actualidad/1446571277_614411.html

proposal of the World Economic Forum in their 2015 Innovation Collaborative Report. stand up (feeding attitudes), startup (starting up, not only companies but new ideas), and scale-up (scale-up with world-class innovation models).

Fig. 12: Cover of the report on education resulting from the E2I2 Forum https://www.raing.es/pdf/publicaciones/libros/educacion_para_la_innovacion.pdf

Educating for innovation and entrepreneurship might be a source of inspiration to create and capture value for the new generations. Also, improving the competitiveness of our companies requires prioritising a change in mentality and attitude of the employees in order to be able to see the opportunities that can be found in problems. Last but not least, fostering the entrepreneurial spirit from childhood to university, and investing in the development of competencies and the capacity and ability to adapt to change.

There is evidence that the most open- minded societies are the most innovative.

The review of educational programmes and methodologies for innovation and entrepreneurship in the classroom that was carried out by the Forum at the Spanish Royal Academy of Engineering raises concerns but also a call to action. The large number of initiatives that have emerged in many schools is the clearest evidence that we are facing a perceived challenge where societal and grassroots solutions are coming from the same base. These fortunate cases must be scaled up.

We can all agree on the importance of promoting education for innovation and entrepreneurship early enough. However, we must make it clear that this does not only pursue the generation of new business people, professionals, and entrepreneurs, but rather shaping the minds of our youth. Also, teachers need to adopt a proactive and participative appetite for change. Because if knowledge can only be transmitted in part, exemplary attitudes are always contagious.

Things will change when the Spaniards and Europeans convince themselves that focusing on this can generate prosperity for future generations and it does not depend on politicians. On the contrary, when the importance of this is recognized, there will be willing political representatives, a subject matter that goes beyond science for scientists and public financing research from general State budgets. Innovation cannot be decreed and it is everyone's business. Much like sports.

Emerging Trends

Beyond the interest that the experiences of the EIT and the discussion at the E2I2 Forum entail for Europe and Spain, it seems that the Great Recession has run parallel with a rethinking of the concept of innovation in the general perception. Starting from the linear view where innovation was understood as an appendix or a result of R&D (eloquently displayed in the Spanish acronym I+D+i as it has been the case also with the European Commission Directorate General responsible for Science, Research and Innovation) innovation is nowadays understood as being increasingly linked to entrepreneurship in many countries, i.e. i&e.

Reflecting upon this evolution, Andrea Renda, then a visiting researcher like me at the EUI and today the new Research Director of CEPS, proposed to form a task force at the end of my mandate at the EIT in 2015. With the title *"Unleashing Innovation and Entrepreneurship in Europe: People, Places, Policies"*, the final report was published in February 2017 and paved the way for a more organic and evolutionary view of the human and social factors of innovation. This trend, also visible in Spain, anticipates a shift that we will examine later, starting with a comparison between the notion of National Innovation Systems and local entrepreneurial ecosystems, where unicorn companies constitute the new proxy of success.

FRACTAL INNOVATION

Fig. 13. Cover page of the report by CEPS *"Unleashing Innovation and Entrepreneurship in Europe: People, Places, Policies"*. https://cdn.ceps.eu/wp-content/uploads/2017/02/TFR%20Innovation%20final.pdf

System or Ecosystem?

As I already confessed before, I believe that whoever understands the dynamics underlying the phenomenon of innovation, will understand the world around us at least a little better. However, it is difficult to target what the central ideas in innovation are, notwithstanding flooded newspapers and publications. Perhaps this is why the first gesture of greatness consists of being humble, recognizing that innovation is complex, both in practice and also for policy. Reflecting upon this complexity, the concept of an innovation system was born in the 1980s.

Luke Georgiou, who was responsible for the evaluation of the Spanish innovation system facilitated by the European Commission in 2014 by the then Minister of Economy and Competitiveness Luis de Guindos, synthetically defined an innovation system as "knowledge, human and financial capital, mediated by institutions." The system is supposed to be made up of a set of interrelated elements: academia, industry, administrations, etc.

In a comparative study of the countries of the European Union, professor Charles Edquist finds that most of them claim to have systemic policies, but very few actually practise them, a linearity captured in the Spanish acronym I+D+i for R&D&I. In any case, the vision of a system is a step forward compared to the orthodoxy of the market failures, as there may also be system failures, all of which justify but might also question public intervention.

On the other side of the Atlantic, Michael Porter, recognized in 2015 as one of the most influential thought leaders by *Thinkers50*, codified the concept of cluster in the 90s as a "geographically close concentration of industries and companies specialised in a given sector." However, this vision, which was so influential in many governments around the world, including the Basque Country and Catalonia in Spain, does not predict how new sectors arise in places with no tradition (Biotech in Silicon Valley and not Boston, for example) or how some countries like South Korea or Taiwan have been able to position themselves so quickly on the global innovation map. This is the criticism of professor Jerome Engel in his book *Global Clusters of Innovation* where he recommends policies based more on behaviours than on ingredients, because it is indeed values and processes that certainly set the course and direction of people and, by extension, of organisations.

Consequently, from systems as a set of connected elements through collaborative R&D or institutional collaboration more generally, we are speaking increasingly about ecosystems. What are the coincidences between both views? Certainly, the emphasis on connections. And the differences? The nature of them regarding scope, subject, and action. While the most widespread analysis unit for systems is national, the ecosystem approach is local, although regional systems fall in between both. The subject in the former view of systems focuses more on institutions versus people as creators of synapses in the dynamics of ecosystems. Regarding action, if public policy has been focusing on financing and coordinating, the job of the 21st century Schumpeterian agencies and policies might rather be to facilitate and orchestrate.

Back to Europe and Spain, structural funds and regional specialisation strategies represent a great opportunity if the temptation to "put old wine in new bottles" is avoided. Because, the pending revolution in innovation and entrepreneurship has more to do with willingness and mindset than with technology or laboratories.

From the Compass to the Map

Perhaps you are not familiar with the world map that is preserved in Burgo de Osma in Soria, Spain, and its *Terra Incognita*, an annotation that has been in use since Ptolemy to emphasise that there is no cartography in unknown lands. This statement makes sense in the world of innovation and entrepreneurship also, which is about, by definition, exploring and exploiting unknown business models or the *terra incognita* for entrepreneurs and researchers also. If there is a strange but fortunate consensus among countries on knowledge as the basis for sustainable prosperity, designing successful policies for innovation and entrepreneurship is not easy. Therefore, not only do researchers have to experiment, but so do the rulers and agencies to make possible what individuals cannot (John Maynard Keynes, "*The End of Laissez Faire*", 1926 cited by Mazzucato in *The Entrepreneurial State*, 2013). We also need political entrepreneurs! We need a convergence of values to adapt business and investment logic to face and solve societal and global challenges.[4]

---

4 See Michael Porter TED Talk: "*Why Business Can Be Good at Solving Social Problems*" https://www.youtube.com/watch?v=0iIh5YYDR2o

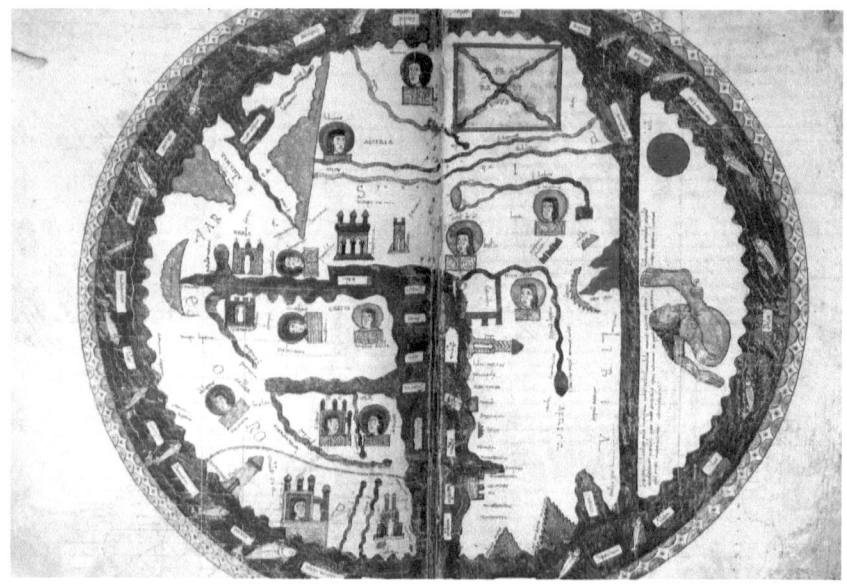

Fig. 14: The world map in the *Beato de Burgo de Osma*, in Soria, including a "patagón" (right below the red spot), that used his only foot to protect himself from the Sun, assuming that beyond the Equator one would find extreme temperatures.

From a bird's eye view, it would seem that Europe is betting all on this because with the 2014-2020 financial perspective of the EU, the European Commission requires all regions that will be managing structural funds to develop an Smart Specialization Strategy (RIS3). In rolling these strategies out, however, there was already a debate confirming that good intentions are not enough. There are two reasons for this. First, the multi-level landscape and governance of Europe's approach to innovation, whereby several regions end up targeting the same areas of biotech, ICT, nanomaterials, etc. The second problem has to do with traditional instrumentation in standard calls for projects that can hardly make any difference.

An interesting evolution to manage complexity and uncertainty regarding next generation policies is the adoption of a double logic, business and investment in the design of innovative public interventions, breaking away from more installed logic of institution and spending. This is the case of the KICs of the EIT or the IP Group and ISIS ecosystems in Cambridge, UK. These initiatives are about leveraging knowledge and technology from public research centres as well as universities through their "third mission" to link them more closely with society. Interestingly, if businesses have always been a key agent of innovation projects, a business logic can also be useful for the implementation of public policies.

What does this all mean? Recall that innovation systems theorists Freeman, Lundvall, Nelson insisted on evolutionary interconnections and interdependencies in systems. Fostering new dynamics around new values is the best compass in this *terra incognita*. Hence the importance of education (the human factor) and communities for innovation (the social factor). After COP 21 in Paris, green economics and net carbon zero could direct ICT, very much like the challenge of migration to the big cities and mass production retrofitted to the Industrial Revolution (see Carlota Perez and Mariana Mazzucato *Innovation as Growth Policy: The Challenge for Europe* in Fagerberg, J., S. Laestadius and B. Martin (eds.) *The Triple Challenge for Europe: Economic Development, Climate Change and Governance* . 2015).

What has Europe been doing in all this? After more than 30 years, it is sad that the EU continues to apply most of the funds to bring partners together or create links through transnational projects where many partners already know each other well. Not to forget the risk of bias with the reputation of the partners involved rather than the excellence of projects per se. Limited by sacrosanct principles of subsidiarity and precompetitive R&D, the limited support that the Commission has given to clusters has been focused on exchanging good practices between hubs that execute their local strategies separately, despite smart specialisation strategies. On the positive side, if Spain piloted Michael Porter's vision on clusters (*The Competitive Advantage of* Nations, 1990), why couldn't we lead the next generation of clusters formulated by Jerome S. Engel (*Global Clusters of Innovation*, 2014) including an international dimension therein that combines links and hubs as a pilot for the EU?

The paradigm shift that we observe in the practice of innovation of companies, from buying (technology) to collaboration (which is the focus of most policies for public–private partnership), suggests a new generation of public policies that are more holistic and dynamic. Adapting the KIC model developed by the EIT at a subnational level, including universities and business schools, and generalising the IP Group and ISIS models would be like using the compass to construct a map, because innovation cannot be programmed top-down. To do this, we must ensure that, like public policies for education or health, innovation is also a citizen issue. We need to discuss and act with the compass of social principles and personal values since innovation is learning through practice. It is knowledge in action.

Unicorns vs. Ecosystems

In the logic of ecosystems and knowledge in action, new business creation is key. Among them, high-growth potential companies (HGPs) have generated a lot of interest due to their contribution to employment, productivity, and economic development. In addition, HGPs can contribute to the emergence of new innovative industries and sectors. Finally, HGPs can be a formidable driver of the innovation system as a whole, revitalising mature sectors. The evidence suggests, however, that HGPs are not more numerous in high-tech sectors, rather, they are found in all sectors. However, the HGPs may have a greater technological content compared with their peers within the sectors considered to be lower technology. For example, IKEA and Inditex have revolutionised the furniture and textile industries, although canonically these are often considered rather mature sectors.

Unfortunately, however, HGPs are problematic targets for investors and policy makers for two main reasons. First, it is difficult to predict which companies will grow rapidly. There are few variables that help predict which companies, on average, have higher rates of growth. Young companies, for example, present higher growth rates, especially in their early years. Smaller companies usually grow faster than larger companies, although there are many large companies that may also become HGPs. Also, evidence shows that the desire expressed by a company's founders to grow is sometimes associated with growth, but not always.

Second, there is very little persistence in fast growth. Even if a company grows rapidly in one year, it is unlikely to repeat it the following year. Of course, repeated rapid growth does happen sometimes, but fast growth is rare and difficult to predict. As a result, scholars have described HGPs as "one hit wonders." (Coad and Leceta, 2017). This is a bit disheartening because this means that by the time you have found an HGP firm, the opportunity is probably already lost as a subject of research, because it is unlikely that the same HGP will continue to grow. In conclusion, growth of HGPs is essentially random and unpredictable.

Such difficulties in predicting which companies will become HGPs and the lack of persistent high growth explain the challenge of investors and policymakers who want to target HGPs. Some variables, such as age, the legal structure, or having a patent improve the likelihood of high growth to a certain extent, so that such firms can create a portfolio of potential HPGs. Mature, smaller businesses which oversee *solo entrepreneurs* have little probability of becoming HPG, so it makes little sense to place them within the same portfolio. Evidence also shows that the increase in the gross amount of new companies does not increase the number of HGPs as there seems to be a balance between the quantity and quality of new companies.

For these reasons, policy makers have also sought indirect approaches to remove barriers to the growth of potential HGPs. This policy is successful but if it encourages all businesses to grow too fast, it could lead them to have financial problems in the event that expansion costs exceed cash flow, which will eventually push them to bankruptcy. Finally, the HGP also plays an important role in relation to other agents (as sources of corporate finance, skilled labour, suppliers, customers, and partners) and activates certain values and attitudes necessary for success (such as an entrepreneurial culture, international ambition, mobility of resources, and alignment of incentives among agents). For all these reasons, it is wise to focus on the larger ecosystem rather than chasing elusive unicorns in vain.

SECOND DISCOVERY: Entrepreneurship Is a Contact Sport

It will be good to take a break, referring back to what I learned during my time at the EIT considering the emergence of the entrepreneurial movement across Europe after the crisis, the Great Recession that began in 2008, precisely the same year when it was decided by the European Parliament and Council to create the EIT. At the EIT, we believed that innovation is ultimately about people, as I pointed out at the end of the first chapter of this book. Another deep learning from that time is that entrepreneurship is a contact sport that requires ecosystems to scale. Moreover, enabling ecosystems that not only transfer knowledge and nurture skills but convey truly entrepreneurial attitudes as well by getting people together.

To illustrate this, I would like to share the story that I used to begin this book with reference to my first newspaper press article as a result of my study grant at the 1991 Summer Session Programme organised in Toulouse, France, by the International Space University (ISU), founded by three entrepreneurial students, including Peter Diamandis whom I have already mentioned. A year later, in 1992, I was an academic assistant in Kitakyushu, Japan at their next ISU summer edition while the Olympics were taking place in Barcelona. By 1991, preparations for the Olympics were already in their final phase and in the minds of all Spaniards.

During the summer of 1991, we, as a group of 120 students from around the world were given the task of designing a permanent living habitat on Mars. With good wisdom, the teachers invited us during the first days to debate the reason for such a mission. Why should humanity invest in such an uncertain and expensive adventure? In group discussions, I remember I made a comparison between the Mars mission and the Olympics. It was a comparison that our supervisor, Wendell Mendel, liked very much and, to my surprise, he quoted it in the plenary. I said that, like the Olympics, a Mars mission made sense not only in the constant search for answers by humanity, but also as a demonstration of the collective will to do so.

In other words, a mission to Mars like that would capture human imagination and catalyse a demonstration of collective will around the world. To support this, I stressed how many countries compete today to organise the Olympic games, realising every four years the dream of what was once just an idea in Ancient Greece. I found it would be very much the same for a future international mission to Mars. Since Europe is the cradle of the Olympics, it is not surprising that more than 2,300 years ago, the Greek Menander of Athens said, "who has the will, has the power." This is why attitudes are so important. But it also explains why, as with the Olympics, entrepreneurship requires teams that catalyse the collective will.

We can also ask ourselves why this phenomenon of entrepreneurship has been slow to emerge yet has particular strength since 2008. Perhaps it is because the crisis has lasted too long, to the point that governments and institutions have shown signs of fatigue and the public budget could no longer afford to support efforts to reactivate the economy. However, citizens and civil societies cannot give up because, if the future is about the younger, young people cannot and will not accept that there is no future, particularly the new generations.

Quite the contrary, I believe that the rise of entrepreneurship largely means an emerging mobilisation of people who want to take the future in their own hands and do so responsibly. On the other hand, this movement is essentially about shaping business models and value propositions bottom up. Also, throughout this movement it seems quite evident that the next generation of innovators goes beyond sectors, disciplines, and geography.

Although Europe possesses all the ingredients for success, there is a widespread mentality of institutional silos. If we want to change our society, we need a great commitment from the universities also in order to nurture talent and educate not only future employees and managers but also future employers and leaders. Because we need more game changers that cut across silos.

I think it is no exaggeration to say that the EIT has contributed to trigger this debate in Europe by insisting that entrepreneurship requires a mind set change in society. In the view of the governing Board, an Entrepreneurial Impact Investment Institute, the EIT, is a new agenda for Europe, integrating the knowledge triangle in the practice of its KICs. By delineating the EIT, the EU institutions were wise to acknowledge that they did not necessarily have the answer in areas as diverse as those of the KICs. As a result, KICs were considerably free to co-create and shape their governance and management structures, including co-location centres.

The need for such centres is consistent with a discovery made by the Hungarian philosopher Michael Polanyi when he summarised *tacit knowledge* saying, "we know more than we can tell." Even in the age of the Internet, human contact is important. KICs manage interconnected ecosystems across borders with co-location centres (innovation hot spots that take advantage of existing capabilities since the EIT could not build them *ex novo* with the limited resources available). Also, they are interconnected in order to accelerate innovation with diversity.

Governance and management of KICs also represented a significant novelty in Europe including a substantial level of experimentation. Inspired by a business logic, KICs are created with a legal status where members elect a CEO whose performance is measured by the results of innovation generated by the community. Also, the relationship established by each KIC with the EIT follows an investment logic, which is based on visible results as well, illustrated in the preceding pages. Ultimately, again, it is about creating end-to-end support (eco)systems where the entrepreneur can interact with professors, researchers, companies, investors, etc.

In short, the strength of the EIT lies in its KICs operations and the strength of their partners. This serves to underline the importance of people as vehicles, not only to develop new knowledge through research, but also for exploitation. Knowledge and impact or knowledge in action is inherent in innovation. We must also discuss the need to demolish the silo mentality and create spaces that are conducive to thinking big, key to revitalising a truly entrepreneurial Europe.

PART III.
REFLECTION: THEORY, PRACTICE, AND THE POETRY OF INNOVATION

FRACTAL INNOVATION

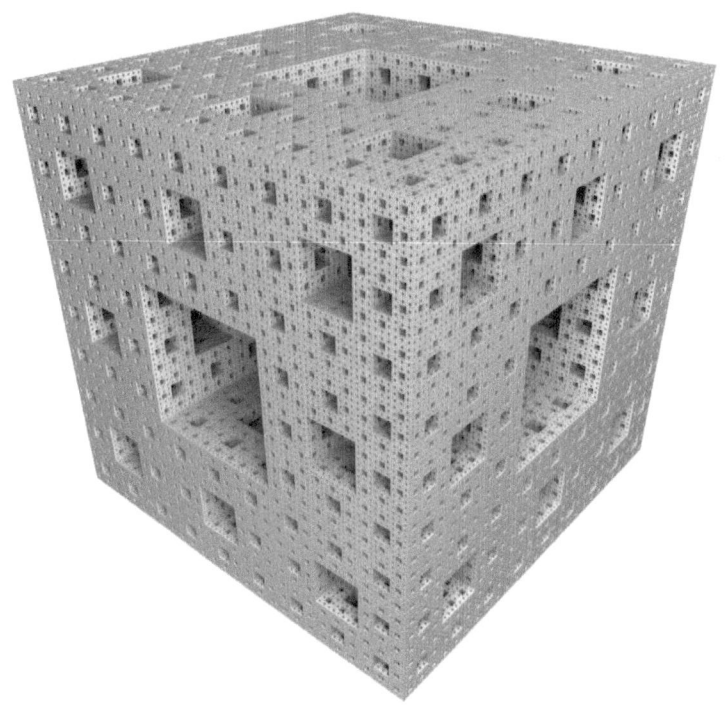

NB Menger's sponge. Like the Sierpinski carpet, it is a three-dimensional generalisation of the Cantor set. Described by the Austrian mathematician Karl Menger (1902-1985) in 1926, it is built from a cube, dividing its faces into 9 squares. From the resulting set of 27 smaller cubes, the central cubes of each face and the central cube are eliminated, leaving only 20 cubes in which the same process is repeated. Menger's sponge is the limit of this process after an infinite number of iterations.

If recovering an entrepreneurial spirit in Europe is critical, the Organization for Economic Co-operation and Development (OECD) acknowledges that fostering new business creation and promoting favourable macroeconomic conditions by governments is not enough. In the search for growth, closer relationships are needed in entrepreneurial ecosystems whose development can be facilitated by smart agencies, like the EIT, which have a willingness to experiment and learn. But to activate an ecosystem, there is no formula and the most successful cases are presented as still photos and ideal situations. Examples being Silicon Valley, Tel Aviv, Singapore, etc. The literature is mute in the causal evolution of world-class ecosystems. We have some clues, however. The main one is that talent is vital and that a successful case often requires an international ambition from the outset.

Today, widespread metaphoric uses of the fashionable term 'ecosystem' appear in academia (MIT ecosystem, for example) but also in the business milieu (General Electric ecosystem). Indeed, from early technology acquisitions to institutional collaborations in R & D more recently, large firms are now exploring new ways to innovate through funds and accelerators. Entrepreneurial universities overwhelm traditional OTRIs using external services such as the IP Group in the UK, which was already cited and investment funds such Karolinska´s in Sweden. Despite the overuse two messages have filtered in from these new dynamics. We have learned that open innovation is here to stay and that disruptive innovation is increasingly present in the minds of incumbents, be they public or private, corporations or universities, as all of them are spurred on by the vertigo and speed of change.

Interestingly, the traditional unit of activity by national innovation agencies such as CDTI in Spain, has been companies and not so much business ecosystems as a whole, although a group of agencies with holistic interventions is emerging. This is the case of EIT and its KICs that we addressed in the previous chapter, the Catapults of the British innovation agency (Innovate UK), the strategic partnerships of its Swedish equivalent Vinnova, as well as the search and support to emerging ecosystems by Business Finland (formerly Tekes) and, even more recently, Canadian so-called "SuperClusters". A key difference is that all these new experimental interventions try to foster more fluid linkages established by people rather than static institutional collaborations canonically driven in projects.

At the beginning of this essay, I emphasised the complexity of the matter at hand by reflecting on a first dilemma of policy makers to reconcile the local nature of innovation with the ambition of entrepreneurs that aim to achieve an international impact. In this chapter, we will find similar tensions at different levels that will help enquire and discuss what relationship can be hypothesised between ecosystems, agencies and talent through, hopefully, next generation innovation policies.

Interestingly, a distinction between mechanistic and organic organisations was formulated in the early 60s by Tom Burns and GM Stalker to analyse the management of innovation in companies. I find that this distinction is very in line with most current literature on policies oriented towards the development of assets vs. behaviours within ecosystems (Porter vs. Engel, which I already cited). And also with agencies that target market failures vs. those targeting system failures, which in turn, end up supporting sustained or disruptive innovations, respectively:

In the logic of mechanistic structures, it makes sense that policies are geared to encourage the specialisation of existing sectors within competitive markets. Once the business models are known, helping to improve their efficiency will be the natural focus of hierarchical business organisations and centralising agencies, that can be named Weberians (Karo & Kattel, 2014) in charge of promoting economic development and updating firms´ capacities.

In the logic of more <u>organic</u> structures, policies are oriented to identify and grow new business models, including those that may be able to create new industries and markets. This is the creative role of new companies that Schumpeterian agencies will push to disruptively "innovate in the periphery" (Breznitz, 2016). And in so doing, to go beyond doing what is needed (improving something) and aim at what might be possible (something new).

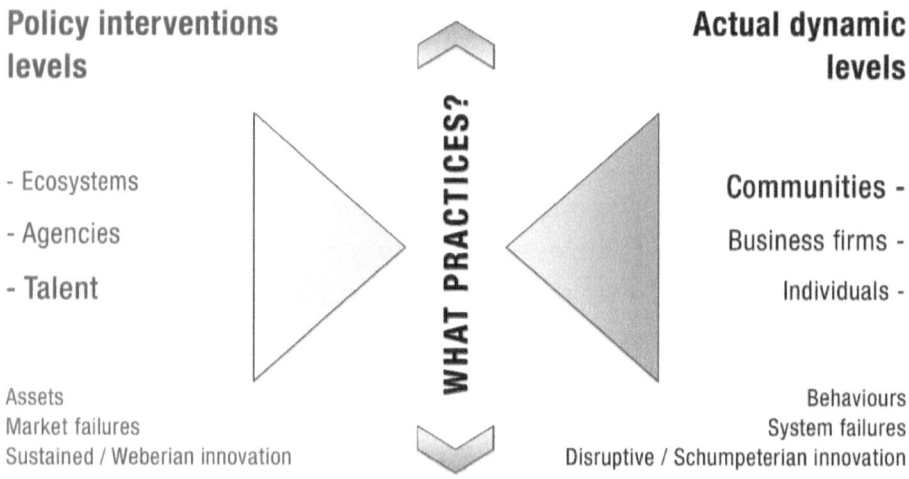

Fig. 15: Tensions between mechanistic and organic structures at the base of different policies for agencies that energise ecosystems. Source: the author.

CRITIQUE

The potential relationship between ecosystems and agencies was the subject of the panel that I organised at the 50th anniversary of SPRU in September 2016. Profs. Mariana Mazzucato, Charles Edquist, Ben Martin, Josep M. Piqué, and the then DG of CDTI, Francisco Marín, participated. In conclusion, I recalled that Aristotle coined the term *poiesis,* in connection with the production or creation of something that did not exist before and has an external end and tangible result, compared to *praxis* (action) and *theoria* (contemplation). The reader will excuse the temptation of the writer to imagine next generation policies for innovation and entrepreneurship halfway between art and science. Therefore, the result of a *poiesis.*

Shifting Paradigms

Science, technology, and innovation have their own characteristics that are sometimes related, but not always. Historically, technology has preceded science. For example, it is obvious that the builders of gothic cathedrals did not have a scientific theory but learned through practice and transferred knowledge through direct engagement between teachers and learners. Also, to innovate successfully, science is not always needed and, as stated before, even when needed, science alone is not enough as we need complementary assets and capabilities to make innovation happen. Since all innovation is a novelty but not every novelty is an innovation, Nobel Prize winner Edmund Phelps, eloquently describes an innovation essentially as an "economic discovery." In other words, an innovative business idea must be accompanied by market success and, ultimately, by economic and societal impact.

However, innovation and science are born both from the will to experiment and the appetite to take risks. And it might be precisely in this experimentation space between academia and business which connects both through the human factor. Unfortunately, it is often forgotten that R&D not only serves to obtain direct results in the form of products and services, but also to educate and train highly qualified human capital, thereby equipping future professionals with the ability to solve problems. This is a fundamental contribution by the scientific system to innovation. Indeed, through R&D, not only disciplinary knowledge is acquired, but critical attitudes are developed to face challenges, whether abstract or practical.

On a macro level, Robert Solow probed as early as the 1960s that US economic growth could not be explained solely by increases in capital and labour, brilliantly coining the residual attributed to knowledge and technology as the "measure of our ignorance". Indeed, there is clear evidence that correlates investments in R&D and economic development. However, causal relationships are more difficult to specify and differ markedly between countries and sectors. This suggests that there are no universal policies and that one must design its own model. What can we do then?

On the one hand, we should avoid the mistake of applying the same type of public interventions to all business sectors regardless of their specific dynamics, ignoring what the effective sources of innovation are according to their corresponding technological intensity. When the crisis in the West began, some spoke of transforming the production model with science or, more headstrong still, that science would get us out of the crisis. Let's recall that R&D, like education or health, requires long-term investments whose effects might come only with time. In the case of Spain, the absence of both sustained policies and the willingness to maintain investments over time will compromise our future development and, in the absence of them, the vulnerability of our economic model will persist.

Second, it is imperative to regularly assess policies, to identify those that work and those that do not in order to make corrections. If ex ante analysis prior to new public interventions is important, even less attention is paid to ex post retrospective analysis of past interventions and programmes. Moreover, it is paradoxical the multitude of new public instruments and plans compared to the unwillingness to critically assess their impact and learn from the successes or mistakes with an attitude of good sportsmanship. In short, smarter *learning by doing* management and more transparent communication are missing in policy, involving all stakeholders, particularly from the private sector whose relative weight in R&D remains limited.

This is not strictly a Spanish problem but a European one. Since the end of the Second World War, the current paradigm that governs innovation policies in most European Union countries has focused on science. A unique case can be found in Sweden where a National Innovation Council was created by the Prime Minister, not science and technology which is the customary scope of many Councils in other countries. Because the acquisition of new knowledge is just one of the ten essential activities in the innovation system following the eminent Swedish and Danish Profs. Charles Edquist and Susana Borrás. Finally, the goal cannot only be to generate knowledge but generate enthusiasm and collective commitment as well, because, as John M. Keynes said, the work of governments is not to do a little better than business, but do what might seem impossible. If you think about it, this is precisely what the public function is about: a vote of confidence by citizens to the State, not only in its ability to manage risks but to reduce uncertainty as well.

The two countries that have dominated the panorama of science (chemistry and physics in particular) historically in the transition from the 19th to the 20th century notwithstanding many differences in their R&D systems are Germany, followed by the United States. However, both have made efforts to create national innovation systems and, more recently, entrepreneurship support ecosystems. Spain must also articulate its diversity with CDTI acting as an 'agency of agencies' and natural meeting point between regional systems and new international trends. Some other innovation agencies around the world are already evolving from the paradigm of the project as a unit of action to systemic and holistic interventions and incentives thus strengthening (eco) innovation systems. The smart specialisation strategies of the European Union and the KICS of the EIT illustrate this transition as they associate not only researchers and entrepreneurs but also university professors and business. Other systemic policies can be found in innovative clusters driven by the Hungarian agency that want to make Budapest the startup city of central Europe, the Catapult centres in the UK, in an economy of intensive services, much like the Spanish economy, but with a university system with international excellence.

As in music, solemn silence comes as a surprise. In Spain, the lack of social awareness about the critical importance of innovation is worrying compared to public support for health and education, for instance. This lack of interest also explains the lack of attention by political parties to remedy the modest progress in the international rankings like the Global Competitiveness Index or the European Innovation Scoreboard. However, transforming innovation policies is a fascinating area for collective action and anticipating the future. We therefore need a social consensus about the importance of more and better knowledge since an innovative nation and State cannot be dictated. The Education, Entrepreneurship, Innovation and Investment (E2I2 Forum) launched by the Spanish Royal Academy of Engineering on April 14, 2015, wanted to trigger precisely such a debate.

I. Provision of Knowledge Inputs into the Innovation Process

- <u>Provision of R & D results</u> and, thus, the creation of new knowledge, primarily in engineering, medicine, and natural sciences.

- <u>Competence building</u>, e.g. through individual learning (education and training for the labour force for innovation and R & D activities) and organisational learning. This includes formal and informal learning.

II. Demand-side Activities

- <u>The formation of new product markets,</u> for example through public procurement of innovation.

- <u>Articulation of new product quality requirements</u> emanating from the demand side.

III. Supply of Constituents for Systems of Innovation

- <u>Creating and change of organisations</u> needed for the development of new fields of innovation. Examples include enhancing entrepreneurship to create new firms and intra-entrepreneurship to diversify existing businesses, and creating new research organisations, policy agendas, etc.

- <u>Interactive learning, networking and knowledge integration</u> among different organisations involved in the innovation processes. This implies integrating new knowledge elements developed in different spheres of the SI and coming from the outside with elements already available in the innovating firms.

- <u>Creation and chance of institutions</u> -e.g. patent laws, tax laws, environmental and safety regulations, R&D investments routines, cultural norms, etc.- that influence innovating organisations and innovation processes by providing incentives for and removing obstacles to innovation.

IV. Support Services for Innovative Firms

- <u>Incubation activities</u> such as providing access to facilities and administrative support for innovating efforts.

- <u>Financing of innovation processes</u> and other activities that may facilitate the commercialization of knowledge and its adoption.

- <u>Provision of consultancy services</u> relevant to innovation processes, e.g., technology transfer, commercial information and legal advice.

Table 6: Key activities in Systems of Innovation, according to Charles Edquist, University of Lund and Susana Borrás, Copenhagen Business School (Borras and Edquist, 2019).

A Clamorous Silence

Faced with the referential position of the US in innovation and the progress made over the last decade by Asian countries, particularly China, the Old Continent does not seem to be moving at the same pace. In 2015, around the early days of the Juncker Commission in Brussels, researcher Reinhilde Veugelers of the Bruegel think tank wondered whether it would be best if Europe gave up the vaunted ambition to become "the most dynamic knowledge-based economy in the world". On the other hand, evidence collected by the OECD shows that countries that limit their action to creating favourable conditions by reforming their fiscal and labour policies while promoting new business creation are not managing to grow.

Therefore, notwithstanding the list of urgent matters for public and private leaders in Europe and in Spain, it is somewhat sad that the meeting of the Ministers of Science, Technology and Innovation at the OECD held in October 2015 in South Korea did not have the proper follow through back here. Moreover, if one considers that the last ministerial meeting of this format took place more than ten years ago, in 2004. And also that in 2015 the OECD innovation strategy developed in 2010, was also formally updated. Yet, the following year, Europe had another encounter with innovation, because in 2016 the European 2020 Strategy (descendent of the Lisbon Strategy) was finally revised and started the mid-term review of the then R&D Framework Programme, Horizon 2020.

In the midst of so much turbulence, the European Union had to focus on short term priorities (refugees, capital markets, etc.), which may help explain why the ministerial appointment did not have a large public impact. However, understanding is not justifying. If vision is an essential feature of leadership, it is even more so in this area, as many long-term challenges knocking at the door of the Old Continent (climate, security, etc.) will only find answers through collective improvement and innovation, as stated by philosopher José Antonio Marina in the 2016 newspaper *El Mundo* (see box below). All in all, in light of the permanent tension between the urgent and the important, let's recall Martin Heidegger when he quoted Plato to claim that "all greatness stands in the middle of the storm."

> *THE MANTRA OF INNOVATION ... Opinion column by José Antonio Marina published in the supplement Ideas of the Spanish newspaper El Mundo, 01/17/2016: Periodically, words appear that seem to hold the key to salvation. One is "innovation." The important thing is to innovate. Innovating, in its etymological sense, is something new. Is it true that everything new is interesting, important, or good? Novelty is not a sufficient evaluation criterion. Some other elements must be added. The canonical text on this subject is the "Oslo Manual", which studies all kinds of innovations but does not include any other criteria other than the diffusion of innovation. The truth is that there are harmful innovations. The economic crisis that we are still suffering from was triggered by destructive "financial innovation." Therefore, setting innovation as a ground rule is a completely stupid position. The important concepts are "improvement" and "enhancement." An innovation that does not improve something is negligible. This, which is valid in the technological, artistic, or ethical world, is also valid in the political world. Not all change is good, not all innovation is to be adored. Only those that pass quality control, that improve something, or that solve a problem more efficiently. The rest is a scam.*

A couple of messages catch the attention positively when comparing the briefings from the 2004 OECD summit of Ministers with the latest in 2015. An evolution that may well reflect the depletion of economic orthodoxy after such a prolonged crisis and the new sensitivities derived from incorporating emerging countries to the OECD, promoted by former Secretary General Ángel Gurria. On the one hand, Governments are now advised by OECD to stop supporting just established companies and to support more decisively the new entrants. Also, they are also recommended to strike a balance between direct and indirect aid. Two issues that deserve special attention in the case of Europe as well as Spain.

The emphasis on emerging versus established companies is explained by both social and economic reasons. Namely, new companies are responsible for a large part of net job creation in most developed countries and, in turn, also of a large share of breakthrough innovations. These companies, in turn, play an important role in national innovation systems, disciplining investments, developing human capital, etc. We should therefore insist that the age of a firm is a better indicator of its innovation dynamics than its size and that not all SMEs are innovative. If most new companies start small, most SMEs are old, as professor Alex Coad stresses.

Regarding direct aid, such as subsidies or soft credits, versus indirect aid like tax deductions, evidence shows that direct support for R&D is more effective to trigger innovation in companies that have not yet innovated, while indirect aid builds loyalty among innovative companies, particularly large companies. On the other hand, another advantage of direct aid is the directionality needed to face grand societal challenges. Consequently, in countries with a medium size domestic but open market, such as Spain, governments must foster sectoral competitiveness as well as to help emerge future sectors that disruptive innovations can create.

What place do Europe and Spain have in this new context? Europe has a comparable supporting infrastructure compared to that of the US for what concerns startups (Telefonica, 2013), however, Europe has a structural deficit in business sectors with medium and high technology in relation to the US as most of the national champions of the Old Continent are in relatively mature sectors.

In fact, the innovation gap of Europe compared to the US is connected to the lack of a sufficiently large number of young leading innovative companies, in ICT in particular. New, world-class technology-based firms are needed to develop national strengths in Europe and compete in a sustainable way in the long term. It might not be surprising that Spain lags behind according to OECD for high-growth companies and, conversely, it is one of the most generous countries for tax breaks for innovation while startups take less advantage of available tax breaks.

One could wonder what could be accomplished by optimising those resources concurrently through direct support in order to explore new sectors and business models that will ultimately benefit the economy as a whole as well as established companies, both large and small? This is precisely the thesis of the World Economic Forum considering the fact that a growing number of corporations are opening up their business models to entrepreneurship and intra-entrepreneurship for disruptive innovation. It is logical that this is the case because future competitiveness in this field is at stake and the threat of disappearing with new entrants is increasingly certain, as evidenced by the declining expectation of the large multinational corporations in the global rankings. In Spain, practically all the Ibex 35 large companies have funds, contests, or accelerators. In short, the paradigm of business R&D is evolving from buying technology to collaboration with research centres and, more recently, the building up of corporate ecosystems.

No More R&D&I

In mid-2016, a curious and unexpected debate took place at the Picasso Tower located at the business district Azca in Madrid during the award for a prize for the best innovation-related study awarded every year by the Accenture-UAM Chair. The debate was motivated by the thesis of the winner, the eminent professor Charles Edquist of Lund University who challenged the composite innovation index that the European Commission publishes annually for all European Union countries, adding a group of input and output indicators (R&D for example).

In the words of the professor, this sum is not a valid measure of the performance of national innovation systems which would be like summing up the kilometers of autonomy of a car with the litres of fuel it can be filled with as a measure of performance. In fact, in 2014 Charles Edquist developed a comparative study of EU countries,[5] showing that most of them declare having a systemic policy, but very few practice it. This is evident in the term I+D+i in Spain (or R&D&I) . To avoid this linearity, Edquist proposes to separate policies for innovation from those for research because he understands that a systemic policy is made up of ten activities that are grouped into four categories (see Table 6 on the preceding pages):

- supplying knowledge inputs for the innovation process (including R & D, education, and training),
- demand-side activities,
- supply elements for the innovation system,
- support services for innovative business firms.

---

[5] https://ec.europa.eu/research/innovation-union/pdf/erac/final_report_from_ session_i_of_the_2014_erac_mutual_learning_seminar.pdf

Unfortunately, too often innovation is understood as a byproduct of science, an approach that has shown its limitations for the European Union as a whole. The figures speak for themselves about how little progress has been made, not only in relation to the US, but also to emerging Asian countries that are positioning themselves much faster. Paradoxically, the visibility that some governments have tried to give innovation policies with the creation of dedicated Ministries often results in focusing on the so-called "R&D sector" that may risk capturing the regulator. So, innovation is confused with science, to end up asking for an increase in public spending for research. It is understood that sectors such as biotechnology or aerospace assimilate all these issues, but we cannot extrapolate science-based innovation to all economic sectors. Comparing the position achieved by Spain in scientific production with its modest position in innovation, it is difficult to understand why we do not recognize once and for all that the linear R&D&I model has not worked.

In the first government of Spanish Prime Minister Mariano Rajoy, it is evident that the Anglo-Saxon model of the BIS Ministry (Business, Innovation, and Skills) adapted to Spain, where R&D&I competences fell under the Minister responsible for economic affairs was not that fortunate. Notwithstanding the effort, Spain failed to achieve a new social contract with science resulting, quite to the contrary, in a rather sad economic contract of science also in public spending. Recognizing the facts would be positive as well as to stress that R&D cannot be a "sector" in the strict sense. This is so as we know for decades now, thanks to the celebrated professor Keith Pavitt of the Sussex University, four patterns of technical change regarding sources, dynamics and effects of innovation for businesses: 1) companies that acquire their technical knowledge from their suppliers, 2) specialised suppliers, especially in the field of equipment and capital goods, 3) scale intensive firms, and 4) science-based companies that innovate in their own R&D laboratories.

In short, Spain is just one example of the paradigmatic change that many Western countries need to operate in order to overcome the linear model. To this end, the OECD recommends "policies for innovation" (plural) since innovation transcends the action of a specific Ministry. Once again science is not always necessary and, even when needed, it is never enough to innovate. The experience in Sweden, points to the creation of a National Innovation Councils instead of the traditional Science and Technology Council, led by the Prime Minister in order to regulate the actions of the government beyond academic or corporate interests. These advisory structures are supplemented by an independent mechanism of evaluation and learning about policy that, in the case of Spain, is imperative.

The Spanish Law for Science, Technology, and Innovation of 2011 included two agencies targeting scientific and business R&D. They are the State Research Agency (AEI) and CDTI. Given that the first absorbed a large part of the competence that the former Ministry of Economy and Competitiveness managed directly through the calls of the Secretary of State for R&D&I, recreating a Ministry of Science and Innovation (which the left party PSOE once decided years ago) or a Ministry of Science and Technology (which the right party PP decided also in the past) would be of little use. On the contrary, we lack a strategic framework that encourages innovation across all Ministries ensuring independent and sustained accountability. At the operational level, the AEI should bear in mind the ERC (European Research Council) and the CDTI assert its mission as an innovation agency that promotes innovation in a broadest sense. Not with funding only, rather as an "agency of agencies" that works strategically together with virtually all Spanish Regions.

An Innovation and Entrepreneurship Council led by the Spanish Prime Minister that would be supported by an office reporting to an independent National Authority could be a better option. In addition, the Royal Academy of Engineering of Spain could implement an independent evaluation mechanism, following the successful model of the US National Academies in Washington. If the unfortunate invention of the term R&D&I (I+D+i in Spanish) is attributed to professor emeritus Fernando Aldana, it is fair to recognize that the Spanish innovation system progressed thanks to the leadership of his OCYT in Moncloa (the site of the Prime Minister residence and office) during the first government of Jose María Aznar. Later, Miguel Sebastián, the chief economist and his team from Moncloa did a lot also during the first term of President José Luis Rodríguez Zapatero.

In short, we must get past the term R&D&I so policies can be more oriented towards results (i&e) rather than inputs (R&D), without confusing reality with desires. Decreeing that all businesses must collaborate with academia is somewhat maximalist. And subordinating innovation policy to research policy would be foolhardy in a country with our industrial structure. There is no reason to prevent Spain from being an innovative country if the government manages to align its actions beyond competences to lead strategies, starting by catalysing everyone's will because, ultimately, the main mission of the public function is to create hope.

INTUITIONS

My professional experience has shown me that first intuitions are the best ones. And also, that the passion to undertake a project is just as important as the courage to discuss the lessons learned later on. Recall that the Greek philosophers postulated that there are three ways to endure. Beyond biology and fame (that for Epicurus was neither natural nor necessary), knowledge. To this end, it is always advisable to ask ourselves what we have learned. What testimonies we can offer to others. Doing so will make it easier to motivate and interest our colleagues.

Indeed, there will be interest in matters that concern us here when we talk about them normally and when we think about how much is at stake in these processes of change that involve innovation, not only technological but social more broadly. In the remaining pages, I would like to address other essential intangibles such as the meaning of leadership, culture, and organisations for innovation. I will address issues at greater length in another book where I intend to discuss the "soul of the machine" or how organisational design fails if there is not a proper culture. Of course, we can ask ourselves to what extent culture is an ingredient or a result of leadership in organisations. So let us begin from this angle. Convinced as I am that the true leader manages people and not tasks, what does it mean to lead?[6]

Passionately Curious

The expression that gives title to this section is by Einstein, but it arose from the presentation of a book on November 2, 2016 at the auditorium of the Rafael del Pino Foundation in Madrid, *El líder ante el espejo* by Antonio Núñez Martín. Steve Jobs essentially said the same thing when he summarised in just a minute and a half his keys to success. Passion and curiosity, coupled with humble determination.

---

6 See my interview with Antonio Núñez published in the economic journal *Cinco Días* published on September 7th, 2016   https://cincodias.elpais.com/cincodias/2017/09/07/el_lider_ante_el_espejo/1504792123_150479.html

Which stresses once again is that when innovation is groundbreaking, the deep motivation of entrepreneurs and researchers are not so different from one another.

From 60 interviews with Spanish CEOs, Antonio reflected in his book about the top ten of their outstanding characteristics and values during turbulent times. The result is a step forward compared to the more customary distinction between transformational and transactional leadership, respectively driven by a willing vision and inspiration or just by execution and results. Neuroscience finds evidence that a single person can hardly be both a visionary and an overseer. The CEO-COO tandem in business faces this duality, although there are no pre-established formulae for the successful division of labour between both.

The debate that followed the presentation of the book with María Garaña, Daniel Carreño, Marcelino Oreja and Tom Burns Marañón was centred on the many challenges faced by leaders in managing multiple tensions: tensions between the short and the long term, orientation to people versus results, global or local focus, etc. And the fundamental difficulty in achieving a dynamic balance.

Antonio used the term "balanced leadership", in line with a then recent article in *Harvard Business Review* (HBR) titled "Both/and Leadership." Balanced leadership, okay, but what kind of balance? Who decides? Unlike in any transaction or transformation, characterised by a previous and a subsequent situation, establishing a dynamic balance requires an underlying arbitrator or principle.

Hence the interest of the formula proposed by the authors of the cited HBR article: separating and interconnecting, in what they come to call *paradoxical leadership*. A thesis close to that of Johan Schot, former director of SPRU in the UK, who says that we live in a world in transition where it is urgent to harmonise personal standing and accepting differences. In other words, to integrate diversity in teams and organisations to navigate the complexity of the world around us.

Something that we all wonder after the dizzying US elections and an unpredictable future may be with Donald Trump back again to the White House. The history of the West is that of advancing principles and fundamental values so we know what to expect. Hence the anxiety of peering into a reality that is no longer variable but contingent, where absolutely everything is negotiable. In such a context, the cited book is great to help us examine the underlying reasons.

Antonio continues with the crusade for leadership in governments, in the path of the *Center for Public Leadership and Government* that he launched at IESE and the Local Leadership Programme with the Foundation Caja Rural de Castilla-La Mancha. *Spain SL* is another of his books where he tries to transfer business paradigms to public service, in line with what Michael Porter proposes to scale successful solutions to major challenges (see footnote 4 in the preceding pages). Along the same lines, the OECD speaks of fluid public-private partnerships with a business logic, from setting up new business models to their accountability.

However, as we have already seen, not all companies innovate and those that do innovate, do so in different ways. Moreover, the dilemma is that, even when doing the right thing, a leader can make mistakes, as evidenced by Clayton Christensen in his book aptly titled *The Dilemma of the Innovator* published in 1997.

Paraphrasing the second part of *Alice in Wonderland* that Lewis Carroll titled *Alice Through the Looking Glass*, perhaps there is room for another book by Antonio, not about the CEO before the mirror, but rather about the CIO (Chief Innovation Officer) through the looking glass because innovation, like life, is a journey.

Culture of Innovation[7]

The above mentioned leading author, Clayton Christensen is, for some at least, the intellectual heir of Joseph A. Schumpeter, who first distinguished between invention and innovation, as the latter means successfully bringing new or significantly improved products or services to the market. This is the role of the entrepreneur which is, by definition, always risky due to the possibility of failure in the development or the uncertain acceptance by a sufficiently large customer base.

So, if there is no impact, there is no innovation, nor can it succeed without relevant knowledge. First of all, sufficient knowledge about the market that opens up a potential opportunity as well as the technical or technological knowledge that allows the actual development of the product or service that makes it possible. The most important thing, like in any human endeavour, is the willingness to take risks and take advantage of knowledge, whether acquired internally or externally.

Technical knowledge may be obtained from experience in production or service provision, while technological knowledge is the result of scientific research to build, improve, or understand technical change. In other words, how to do things. Only technological knowledge and technology are the result of a systematic search through research and development (R&D) that can be executed also by business firms. R&D can be executed, managed or funded by the same company or other institutions that will licence the technology. In any case, the company must have sufficient tacit knowledge to understand and apply the acquired technology.

---

[7] The text corresponds to the article jointly written with Juan Mulet and published on October 2, 2016 in the Spanish newspaper *Cinco Días*

Thus, R&D is a fundamental part of the complete innovation process that companies may carry out themselves or not. But it is true that the company that carries out R&D would have a greater advantage because it will be able to generate its own technology and will capture a larger part of its added value. What is becoming more important every day, it will also be better able to monitor and understand the technologies available or new in the market. This is the so-called "absorptive capacity" or the two faces of R&D, innovate and learn, postulated in 1989 by Cohen and Levinthal. Between buying or developing, innovators must do both.

From a business point of view, however, innovation and R&D are not necessarily linked. There may be very innovative companies without R&D and others which are research intensive but are not innovative because they do not bring new products or services to the final markets directly, rather they commercialise the technology they generate. Such is the case of specialised suppliers in capital-intensive sectors. In the knowledge economy, R&D and innovation are important for the welfare of countries and are the subject of attention by all governments. An attention that must differentiate between two very different realities. Indeed, R&D is strongly conditioned by the adventurous spirit of researchers and their motivation to offer society more and better knowledge that is, by definition, new to the world. While innovations are determined by the priorities of the markets, both existing and new ones, and are disruptive for a company's own business model but not necessarily because of the radical technologies involved in making goods and services competitive. Businesses' main motivation is the expected economic benefits.

Traditional economics acknowledge the existence of market failures that justify public support for R&D. The practical impossibility of preventing new generated technologies from being used by others who have not participated in their development, the great uncertainty associated with the development processes and the high costs associated with this activity are additional reasons for governments to do so particularly when the R&D is carried out by businesses. Often, however, public R&D efforts end up with technologies that are potentially useful, but are not used in innovations as they can also become obsolete and replaced by new ones. An R&D incentive policy is a necessary but not sufficient condition for innovation.

Pondering the unquestionable success of Japan in the 80s, Chris Freeman, founder of SPRU at the University of Sussex in the UK, the longest standing innovation research centre in the world, stated that the leading countries have a higher quality of their national innovation systems. A quality that would be determined by their ease and ability of converting available science and technology into a competitive offer to the world. This can be measured by progressive increase in the number of innovative companies and the intensity and ambition of those that already innovate. The essential agents in an innovation system are indeed the businesses, consequently key policy instruments should encourage companies, both existing and new, to take risks to innovate. However, considering the difference among countries beyond aggregate support to business R&D, some economists talk about system failures within the policy mix of governments.

Eurostat confirms that the highest percentage of companies in Spain that declared themselves as being innovative is less than 30%, while in Germany it is close to 70% and both France and Italy are close to 50%. It is also worth noting that, over the years, this percentage has practically remained unchanged. Before the Great Recession, for instance, the Spanish National Statistic Office (INE) registered that the percentage of Spanish companies that carry out R&D activities remained at just over 5% between 2004 and 2014, while that of companies that declare themselves innovative and that, in turn, also carry out R&D activities, doubled from 24% in 2004 to 48% till 2014. These figures suggest that although the policy to encourage R&D in businesses may have had effects, the percentage of innovative companies has remained stable. Moreover, the total number has probably decreased given the sharp reduction in the number of business firms caused by the crisis. In summary, promoting R&D by the government was not enough to ensure that innovation is incorporated into the strategy of more firms. This is a systemic challenge not just for Spain taking into account that the OECD has been recommending governments to design whole-of-government innovation strategies since a more than a decade. If innovation is more than R&D and promoting it also requires much more subsidies, the ultimate challenge of next generation strategies is to create the culture enjoyed by truly innovative countries.

Agendas or Agencies?

The Spanish philosopher Ortega y Gasset wrote at the end of his introduction in *Reflexiones sobre el Quijote* that, "isolated criticism is impiety. The pious and honest man acquires, when he denies it, the obligation to create a new affirmation. Or, at least to try it." This chapter wants to pay off the debt acquired with my article of June 21, 2016, in the newspaper *Cinco Días,* which I titled "No More R&D&I", motivated by the hopes and dilemmas that the then new government was facing.

To begin with, let's recall that Harvard professor Clayton Christensen, intellectual father of disruptive innovation, warned that if a company wants to innovate in an unconventional way, sometimes it might be more appropriate not to listen to its current customers and invest in lower-performance products which, in the long run, can end up being much more successful. Also, the "political entrepreneur" who intends to innovate policies for innovation faces a similar dilemma. Satisfaction of the beneficiaries of public aid is not enough if it does not want to renounce to emerging new sectors. It is therefore necessary to continually experiment, learn by doing, and evaluate the impact. However, this is not an easy task while complying with the rules and expanding the boundaries of public action.

Investigating successful innovation policies in Israel, Finland, and Ireland, professor Daniel Breznitz, expert in innovation agencies of fast growth, shows that the greatest impact from innovation may come from the periphery, through agencies with small budgets and sufficient autonomy. In other words, "Schumpeterian agencies" outside the public and political attention. In the same way that more and more companies enable sandboxes (funds, accelerators, etc.), for more than two decades now since Mind Lab in Denmark was set up, a worldwide movement has emerge to catalyse governmental creativity by codifying the expectations of citizens, their needs and, ultimately, future demand. Innovating is complex and, precisely for this reason, we need new and experimental approaches.

Stimulating the demand and capacity building in those new agencies will be necessary to implement Mazzucato's entrepreneurial State. Indeed, there is nothing to prevent the public from being creative and innovative like businesses. On the contrary, there are emerging paradigms in the most advanced countries that are trying to capture the new dynamics of business. One sees progress, from the purchase of technology to R&D collaboration as well as to exploring more open and disruptive forms of innovation. Likewise, new policies for innovation evolve from science-based innovations to public-private collaboration (which is where most public support is) to experimentation and exploration in ecosystems.

In the task of building ecosystems with talented and international ambition, Spain has several agencies in charge of research, innovation, and digital agenda that are aligned with similar organisations in Europe. This is a new situation that also represents a great opportunity to place Spain at the same level as other countries. Empowering those agencies will free the general administration of the State from its daily management of aids and allow Ministries´ work to be oriented to the design and evaluation of strategies and policies in new trends and agendas like:

- **Educate for Innovation and Entrepreneurship.** While the connection between research and innovation is very consolidated (perhaps too much so if we want to overcome the linear model), the relationship between education and innovation is about to explode because human capital is the main product of universities and the most effective way to transfer knowledge. We must inspire not only the attitude of students, but that of the teachers as well. In short, we need new research and education, which requires new spaces of co-creation with the business world and society to develop entrepreneurial abilities and an innovative culture in academia.

- **Open Innovation and Intra-entrepreneurship.** Open innovation can extend the horizon of possibilities of businesses, including customers, suppliers and even competitors in their own sector as well as other companies, both new and established in existing and new markets. Spain has large companies (networks, logistics, services, etc.) that may particularly benefit from open innovation and collaboration with startups and spin-offs. In turn, we must imbue an innovative culture and intra-entrepreneurship to established companies, both large companies and SMEs.

- **Radical and Disruptive Innovation.** The promotion of world-class innovative products and services is imperative and urgent in order to reduce the worrying business deficit in medium and high technology sectors (radical innovators) and business models (disruptive such as GAFA: Google, Apple, Facebook, Amazon). Both Europe and Spain have a deficit in technological intensity of their companies compared with the US, which is one of the keys to Europe's trans-Atlantic innovation gap. Also, platforms play a determining role to help scale up new businesses in global markets.

The three topics above focus on processes and not on specific inputs such as R&D or public subsidies. This is consistent with the fact that are complex phenomena and the best way to attack them is to focus on the processes and not on the outcomes since we are unaware of potential target sectors and innovative firms that new technologies will make possible. It is time to launch wide-ranging debates. Already at the dawn of what came to be called the Information Society (a field that could not be easily located in any organisational chart of the Spanish government), Minister Josep Piqué arranged a panel of experts that formulated a strategy and crystallised a structure in the paradigmatic Secretary of State SETSI.

Regarding Spanish agencies responsible for capability building with supply policies, the State Research Agency (AEI) with the European Research Council (ERC) and CDTI with the European network of national innovation agencies (TAFTIE) can find many good practices. At the same time, Red.es is the reference agency for the extensive use of ICTs in public services but also a meeting point for digital transformation of lagging sectors (industry, energy, pharmaceuticals, and health, according to a report by Roland Berger for Siemens). The manifesto "Scale

Up Europe" presented to European Commission in September 2016 was a good starting point to inspire new instruments at EU level like the European Innovation Council (EIC) which also stimulated more recent developments in Spain like a StartUp Law to leverage on entrepreneurial boom in Europe to inspire potential world-class cases. In short, digital transformation can be used as a pilot to innovate and launch next generation policies for innovation and entrepreneurship.

FINALLY: Like Life, Innovative Entrepreneurship Is a Journey

The philosophy of history and the theory of organisations strive to identify patterns of change. For example, in 2007 Frank W. Geels and Johan Schot, whom I have already alluded to with their proposal to apply "historical imagination" to the complex times in which we live, postulated *socio-technical systems in transition* that insist on the technical and social change that every innovation entails. Changes that first appear in "niches" then in "regimes" and end up altering the "landscape".

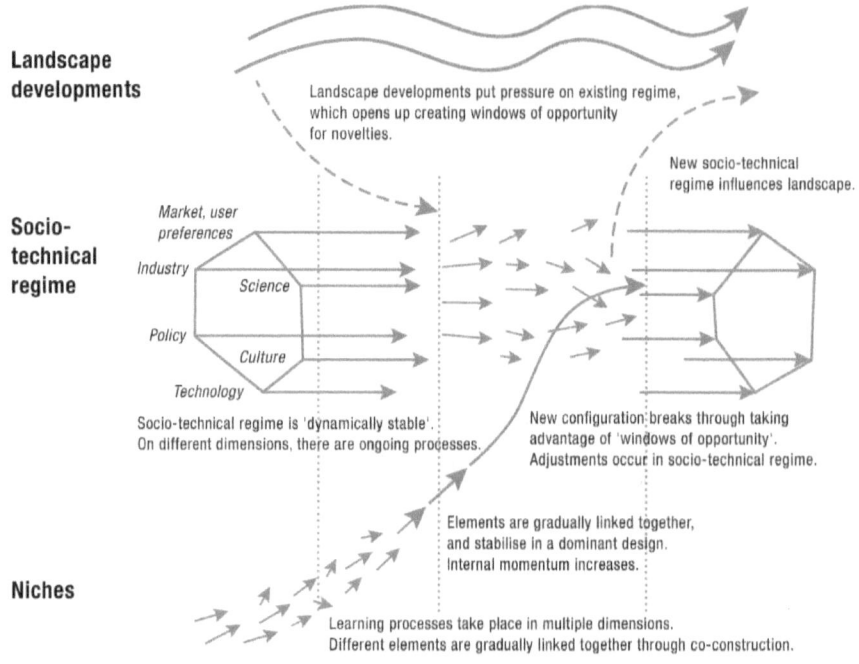

Fig. 16 A schematic view of the theory of systems in transition according to its seminal authors, Frank S. Geels and Johan Schot.

Interestingly, this is also the difference between radical (technology) and disruptive (also social) innovation that postulates Clayton Christensen depending on the degree of acceptance that the new developments end up achieving. This is because the ability of the user groups to adapt is largely overtaken by the pace of the possibilities offered by many new technologies. There are two ways to innovate disruptively: create <u>new markets</u> with users who do not consume today or serve those who are <u>overserved</u> and will accept more accessible and affordable offerings.

THE DISRUPTIVE INNOVATION THEORY

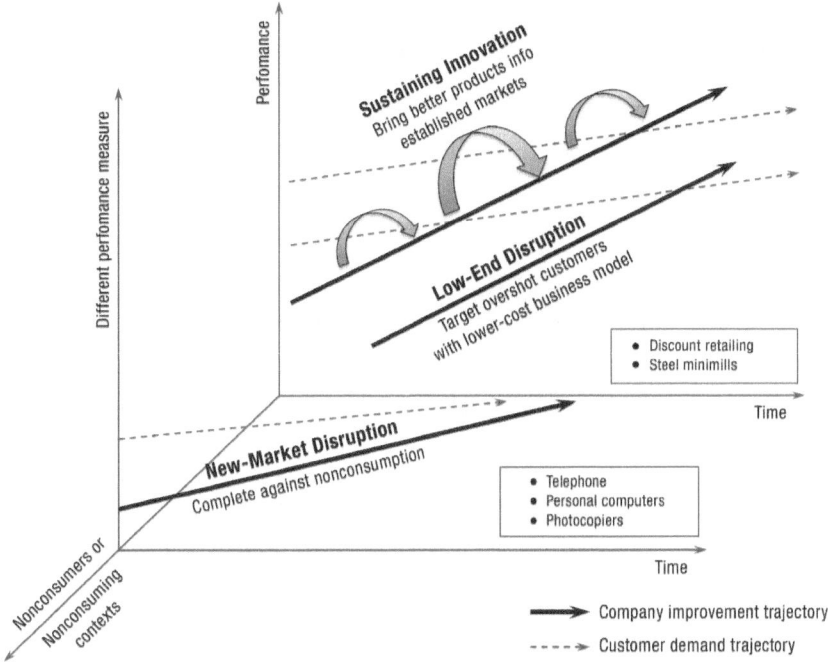

Fig. 17 A synthetic view of the two forms of disruptive innovation (new markets and more accessible and affordable products) according to Clayton Christensen.

Thus, by definition, disruptive innovation must be simple, even though it may not necessarily be easy nor straightforward. In this regard, professor Daniel Isenberg from the Babson College defends "contrarian entrepreneurship", convinced that entrepreneurs in adverse conditions are precisely those who see opportunities in the obstacles. Remember that every innovation requires the combination of an idea (technology) and acceptance (user). However, innovation requires much more than R&D. Otherwise, we could ask ourselves like Ortega y Gasset, who asked himself that if progress (innovation) results only from the sole advancement of reason (science), why does it take so long? Let us make this the theme of our time, because innovation means change and something everyone can and should foster. It is something that next generation policies should accelerate.

For instance, events such as those organised by the Singularity University (the first European summit held in Budapest in 2013, where the EIT HQ is located), was attended not only by "geeks" but also by executives, authorities, and professionals, independently of their affiliations, institutions and origins in their will to approach innovation differently. The overall message conveyed to these potential entrepreneurs is similar to the message that has also become popular in Spain also with the growing population of entrepreneurs: be and believe in yourself.

Why be ourselves? The popular TED Talks are good illustrations that everyone has something to say, one just has to choose the topic that motivates him or her. Also, I do not believe there is a person who has come to this planet thinking that life is just about survival. Until very recently, the image of entrepreneurs was associated with the need to search for financing in order to start a new business for his or her personal success. Interestingly, social entrepreneurs are also being heard, including young people who want to make the world a better place. All of this is both indicative and encouraging of the change in mentality that is taking place.

Why believe in ourselves? Convictions change perception and by changing perception, we change reality. "To believe it is to create," as the great agitator of minds a century ago in Spain, Miguel de Unamuno, said. Moreover, Ortega y Gasset would find that the radical principle of existence is neither about our mind nor the world around us, but life. People are the reason for EIT and vice versa. Events like the EIT summit (INNOVEIT), in which students involved in the KICs are actively participating, enliven the Institute and enabled their countries of origin to take part in the experience. Innovative entrepreneurship, like life, is a journey.

Despite the coincidences that both EIT and Singularity University share and mean for a new commitment to innovation and entrepreneurship, it is interesting to note that while the Singularity University puts more emphasis on exponential technologies, the EIT focuses on talent, particularly in young people, as the best promise for the future. Both agree on the importance of inspiration, thinking big, and outside the box to exploit the *terra incognita*, beyond what is already known.

Like Peter Diamandis I believe the most promising factor is the 3 billion new minds that are on the horizon and that the digital revolution will connect. We live in an era of opportunity if we face the challenges in a constructive and collaborative way. As in any adventure, we can see it as a threat or an opportunity. The surprise is that living with passion increases the chances of success. It is not Don Quixote who says that, but Sancho Panza. In this duality lies the key to the complexity that we observe and the diversity that we must be able to manage in order to succeed.

In all this, perhaps the brain, our way of thinking and feeling is the best compass that we can use to face the challenges ahead. To that end, we need to connect, not only to complement each other, but also to activate social trust in the way we work, live, and enjoy ourselves. There is no success without passion, but there is also no passion without pleasure. To this we dedicate the concluding chapter.

IN CONCLUSION:
Mirrors, Lenses, and Prisms

No doubt that identifying patterns of change would be very useful to identify the necessary skills and the most suitable professional profiles to maximise the success of organisations and teams. Along these lines, if many consider management books to simply be "airport literature," neuroscience begins to confirm ideas from sociology and psychology that have anticipated our knowledge about how we relate to one another and how we are. What if, as with fractals, there were underlying structures at different levels? This is my thesis. That, like fractals, there are underlying regularities also in innovative teams and organisations.

To unravel structural patterns, we use a theory well known in business schools called the 'competing values framework' initially proposed by Robert E. Quinn and John Rohrbaugh in 1983. This theory is used to measure the effectiveness of organisations in general resulting from the composition of two dimensions. First internal orientation to the inside versus external orientation towards the outside of the organisation. Second, stability and control versus flexibility and change. By combining both, four models are created. These models are: create (new things), compete (work fast), control (done properly), and collaborate (work together).

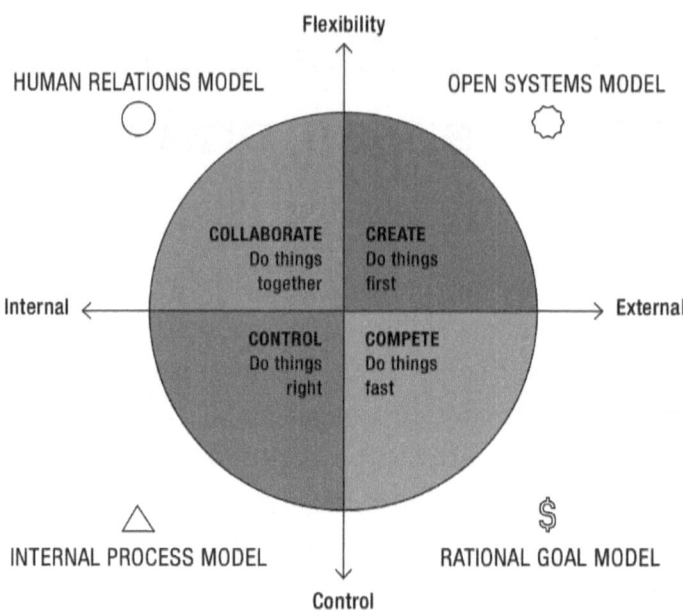

Fig. 18: Quadrants and models resulting from composing the two dimensions in tension of the Competing Values Framework formulated by Robert E. Quinn and John Rohrbaugh initially in 1983.

The first model (create) is characteristic of open systems capable of adapting and attracting external resources for innovation and creativity. The second is about setting rational goals (compete), putting the emphasis on action, planning, and establishing objectives and efficiency. The third (control) focuses on internal processes, hierarchy, measurement, and information management. Finally, we have collaboration, where human relationships are based on cohesion and morality with an emphasis on training and the belief that people are not isolated individuals, but rather members of a cooperative social system pursuing a common interest.

Let us now compare the framework with the 'four thinking styles' proposed by neuropsychologist Katherine Benziger with insights by Carl Gustav Jung from 1921, that I was introduced to by my insightful, generous and wise Executive Leadership Coach, Prajna Paramita, during my term at the EIT. The styles assume that we are different to the extent of what our brains are, something that the Benziger test can identify in a few minutes. This is such a groundbreaking tool that some companies use it when recruiting managers. Thus, the right frontal quadrant, in which intuition is located, is where imaginative and creative tasks, adaptability, etc. are established. The left frontal quadrant (thought), is where we set goals, evaluate reality, and make decisions. The posterior left (detection), identifies sequential tasks, routines, detailed processes, etc. Finally, the right posterior (feeling), excels at building relationships and harmony.

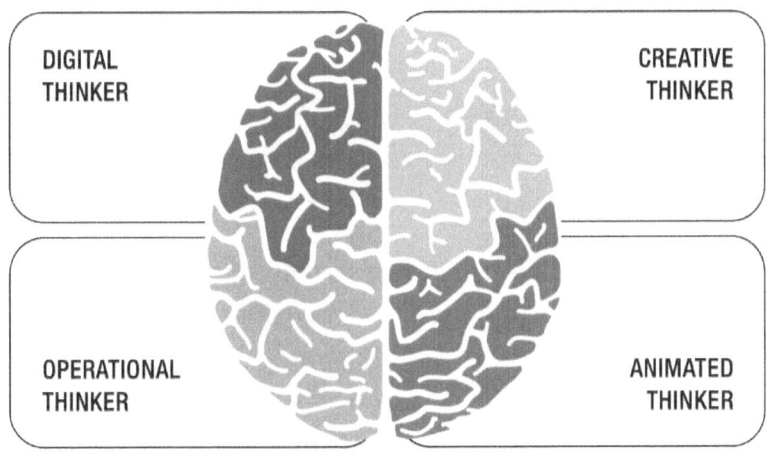

Fig. 19: Katherine Benziger's four thinking styles in a simplified view of their correspondences with the human brain. See http://www.benziger.org/ and BTSA (Benziger Thinking Styles Assessment) that can be easily found on the Internet.

So, our brain seems to reflect the competing value framework as well. Would these same dynamics be those with which teams function as well? Let us imagine the framework of competing values as **a mirror** where we can observe ourselves to assess leadership in business organisations. Also structured in four zones, each key person is stronger when creating, structuring, executing, or communicating.

This is precisely what a full business or start up team is asked to do with a CEO (Chief Executive Officer), COO (Chief Operating Officer), CFO (Chief Financial Officer), and CCO (Chief Communication Officer)!

What lessons can we draw from this for entrepreneurship? First of all, confirming a frequent mistake that can ruin a new company when scaling it up if all the founders have the same profile. Another, perhaps even deeper lesson is that the passion for entrepreneurship must be accompanied by humility, recognizing one's own limitations and capabilities, and consequently, the need of others. This was the second part of the famous recipe by Steve Jobs who, beyond loving what you do, recommended also to surround oneself with complementary people and talents.[8] Ultimately, that is how we are and how we relate to one another.

Precisely, as a humble engineer, I wonder if neuroscience may be setting up the basis of the social engineering that the XXI century requires. On the other hand, as the fathers of neuroscience, Santiago Ramón y Cajal, warned, "Ideas don't last long. You have to do something with them." This is so as innovation is knowledge in action. And this is relevant to people too. If we use the competing values framework not as a mirror but as **a lens** through which to observe organisations, we understand the point of view of professor Jeff DeGraff.

The most synthetic and profound video I know is that of Steve Jobs: *The Secret of Success* https://www.youtube.com/watch?v=PznJqxon4zE You can't say more in less than two minutes. You need passion but, equally important, you also need to integrate and manage diversity to navigate complexity in work and life.

Starting with the competing values framework, DeGraff developed what he refers to as the *innovation genome* and more recently renamed the *innovation code*[8] that he considers applicable at three different levels: the configuration of startup teams, the analysis of organisations (business firms in particular), and any complex social phenomenon more generally. To this end, he analyses the four forms of leadership in pairs, which he attributes to the artist, the athlete, the sage, and the engineer, resembling the thinking styles of Bezinger. Anyone who has faced the challenge of teamwork in business and startups would agree with the imperative of managing diversity resulting from very different profiles. Something that DeGraff understands associates to 'constructive conflict'. Hence the importance for leaders and managers to know their type of leadership and corresponding ability to:

> **Create:** The artist is intelligent and creative. He expects change, so his influence is based on anticipating a better future and generating hope in others. He is original and imaginative, capable of handling a high degree of ambiguity and abstract ideas. His success is defined by expressing new ideas and prototyping those ideas when possible.
>
> **Compete:** The athlete is aggressive and determined. Objectives and goals are actively pursued in competitive situations. Winning over competitors is her primary goal.

---

8 https://www.psychologytoday.com/ca/blog/innovation-you/201710/what-attributes -are- key-successful-leadership https://www.youtube.com/watch?v=_LYsH6XU584&-feature = youtu.be

These leaders are tough drivers and producers, they are very demanding of themselves and, by extension, of others. Speed, stealth, and discipline are key as well as exercising power.

Collaborate: The sage is loving and empathetic. Aware of others, he cares about the need and importance to build a community and to do that, he shares knowledge, manages conflicts and makes decisions by consensus. He creates solid relationships through dialogue, trust, and understanding. In return he obtains results in terms of shared values and commitment. He thus pursues morality and collective commitment.

Control: The engineer is a well formed, expert technician. She is diligent and meticulous. She influences others through control and information. She improves efficiency through process redesign and reliable technology. Success consists in improving quality by using different processes. She is averse to risks and seeks to eliminate variations in the system, valuing standardisation and consistency. Measurement is used as a tool.

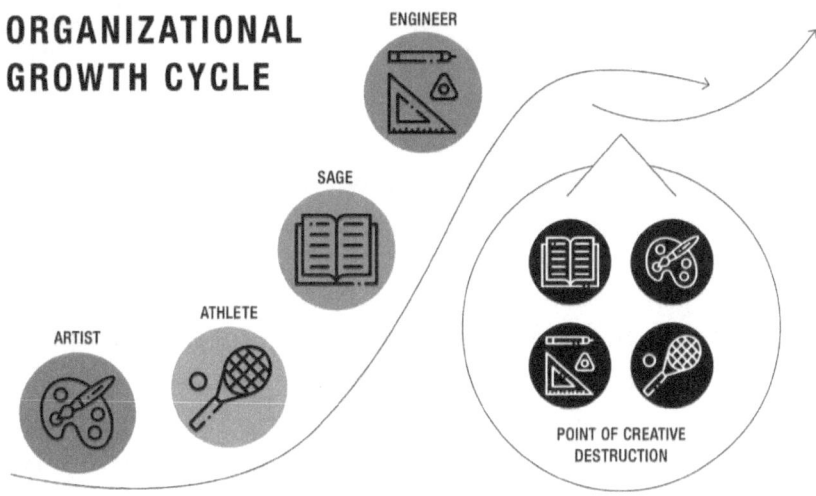

Fig. 20: The four leadership styles (artist, athlete, sage, and engineer) in their relationship to the organisational growth cycle according to Jeff DeGraff's innovation code.

Leaders must have an open mind to know their weaknesses and collaborate with others who challenge them in diversity. This is so because managing diversity will be critical to achieve a positive growth cycle. Sages and engineers challenge each other, as do engineers and artists, but great leaders will develop the right culture, engaging environment and competence in their company or organisation by orchestrating the desired value proposition. Unfortunately, leaders may often favour practices that closely resemble their own preferences rather than changing those practices to suit the situation, to the detriment of the organisation. Lack of insight and experience about when you need to recruit others will not yield the optimal result. All of this means managing tensions that DeGraff sums up like this:

"When you combine the radical and visionary thinking of the artist and the methodical and practical thinking of the engineer, you get revolutionary and manageable innovation. Very ambitious but without high risk. When you combine the ruthless and results-oriented attitude of the athlete with the conscientious and value-oriented attitude of the sage, you get an innovation that is both a good investment and good for the world."

Let us now analyse the ecosystem using this same **prism**. This is the highest level of analysis in the innovation genome/code by DeGraff. Unfortunately, regarding the practical building up of innovation ecosystems, the literature is silent if not sceptical as to how assets and behaviours should be combined over time. Take for example the book *Boulevard of Broken Dreams: Why Public Efforts to Boost Entrepreneurship and Venture Capital Have Failed and What to Do About It* by Harvard professor Josh Lerner. Also, Babson, the college number one in entrepreneurship and professor Daniel Isenberg recall that a vibrant entrepreneurial ecosystem is characterised by six dimensions or components, namely: policy, finance, culture, support, human capital, and markets. However, as indicated above, a recipe is not just a collection of ingredients.

Responding to a challenge from the Columbian city of Manizales, the Babson College had the opportunity to demonstrate that their teachings are not only theoretical using the methodology developed by professor Daniel Isenberg in order to scale up entrepreneurial ecosystems. The result is one of the few practices documented in the literature, precisely about the partnership between Babson College and Manizales. A paper published in the *MIT Review* in 2016 explains the transformation of the city into a successful ecosystem in a relatively short span of time. Today, Manizales is a success story in the region, recognized by the World Bank whose website contains a testimony of the former President Santos, a case that other countries and regions may want to try and emulate.

The said paper, "*Fostering Scale Up Ecosystems for Regional Economic Growth. Innovations Case Narrative: Manizales-Mas and Scale Up Milwaukee*" draws attention to the fact that the proposed methodology revolves around four steps, which in turn recalls the four styles that DeGraff talks about and, by extension, the four quadrants of the competing values framework, applied this time not to a team or to an organisation but an overall community like Manizales. These steps are 1) activating partners, 2) aligning leaders, 3) establishing an execution platform and proof-of-concept programmes and 4) systematising and expanding programmes and local capacities. This is a relevant case for the alchemy of catalysing wills and assets within the broader social scope of a community that targets a vibrant ecosystem.

This concludes our tour around the optics of **mirrors, lenses, and prisms**. The attentive reader could relate the two dilemmas presented briefly in the preceding pages when I insisted that managing tensions and looking for an optimum with next generation policies and programmes for innovation and entrepreneurship. What dynamics result from juxtaposing the dilemma of the first chapter (local nature of innovation against a global ambition of its impact) with that of the third (doing things right that we already mechanically know or trying new ones more organically)? The composition of both dimensions or tensions would result in a two-by-two matrix, with an even closer meaning since the associated dilemmas are even more profound. On the one hand, a reality that accompanies us throughout our lives and that is the borderline, be it real or just perceived, between oneself and the rest of the world. Myself and my circumstance following Spanish philosopher Ortega y Gasset. On the other hand, the opportunity to do just what we now understand or, alternatively, to project ourselves and try to make the desirable also possible. That is to say, power and knowing versus wanting and experiencing.

In my view, it is difficult to think about any human or social phenomenon that cannot be assessed against this double dilemma or decision matrix, simple and complex at the same time, determining what is inside or outside the horizon of ambitions of each of us and, on the one hand, deciding to continue doing the same or something different. Even love could be examined against these questions, which explain how we are and how we relate to one another. The same can be said concerning teams and organisations. When at the EIT in Budapest I used to reflect about the human and social factors of innovation, I imagined the triangle of knowledge as the ecosystem or the circumstance of the entrepreneur with passion as his driving force. That is why those that love us recommend us to follow our heart, something to keep in mind in our personal and professional trajectory, navigating the complexity around us since "nothing great in the world has ever been accomplished without passion", said Hegel. I hope the reader will excuse the temptation to think and communicate in images, which I find so stimulating.

A close example from my recent professional career is the strategy approved by Red.es to activate the talent of its own staff and open up to the ecosystem of public and private partners. A strategy that will have, perhaps, more life than their creators imagined thanks to the strategy provisions to learn from implementation and thus, to accommodate its potential evolutions to future contexts in which Red might need to operate. As displayed in Fig. 21, the strategy is structured along four pillars which recall the competing values framework as well, in between internal-external orientation and flexibility-control. And, by extension, the double dilemma that we discussed above is also relevant here, namely, that of local vs. global ambition of innovations, combined with mechanistic vs. organic dynamics in the organisation.

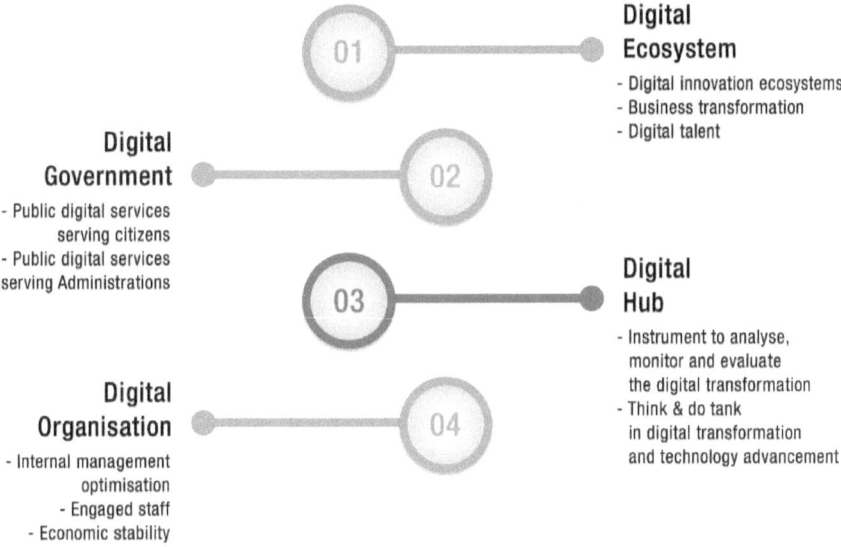

Fig. 21 Synthetic vision of Red.es strategy 2017-2020. See https://www.red.es/redes/sites/redes/files/Plan_Estrategico_red.pdf

In conclusion, I would like to position the preceding discussion in the light of the paradigmatic Interuniversity Master in Economics and Innovation Management (MEGIN) here in Spain, jointly run by the Complutense, Autonomous and Technical Universities of Madrid. Specifically, the view of professor José Molero, who used to arrange the business assets for innovation in three concentric circles, which are the firm itself, other functions that it needs to successfully bring an innovation to the market and, finally, the context in which it is located. If there are underlying structures that are reproduced at different levels when innovating, they should definitely be found within these three concentric circles. Comparing the quadrants of the frames we have seen, the conclusion appears to be as follows:

Frames	Mind (Bezhinger)	Firm (DeGraff)	Ecosystem (Isenberg)	Ecosystem (Isenberg)
Create	Creative mind	Artist	Activate	Disruptive innovation
Compete	Digital thinker	Athlete	Align	Sustained innovation
Collaborate	Animated Thinker	Sage	Manage	Radical innovation
Control	Operational Thinker	Engineer	Systematize	Incremental innovation

Table 7: Conceptual summary of the conclusions and central thesis of the book: competing values, thinking styles, teams and ecosystems and their hypothetical link.

If there are underlying structures and dynamics common to these different levels, the higher the ambition of the innovative project, the more important the entrepreneur's ability to integrate and manage diversity in the team should be. For this reason, the humility of a leader is as paradoxical as it is advisable. This is my experience and conviction in choosing between local or global knowledge in action and doing only the right thing or attempting to possibly innovate more disruptively. These tensions resonate, in turn, with the two dimensions of the competing values framework (internal or external orientation, flexibility or control). Perhaps these resulting quadrants are not so far from the four canonical ways to innovate that are found in the literature: disruptive, sustained, radical, and incremental (Table 7).

Nothing can compensate for one's own experience, however, as it is up to the entrepreneurial innovator himself or herself to see and translate the complexity of the world and the challenges of life into opportunities. Already at the beginning of this navigation,

I pointed out that any journey is ultimately personal. Let´s then keep it up by celebrating that we are the future, since we indeed are essentially what remains to be done, rather than what we have done so far. And also, that it is up to each one to preserve the fascination of those who see things for the first time.

Note about the author

by Alfredo Sánchez,
CEO of Inspiralia

I met José Manuel during a special year. A year in which he was relegated from his post as International Director of CDTI in 2010 (where he served for 6 years after 12 more years with the European Space Agency, totalling 18 years!).

I am a businessman and Inspiralia, my firm, is dedicated to helping our clients in their technological development from idea to industrialization. I knew of the success of the International Directorate of CDTI, especially in helping Spanish companies, including SMEs, attract European funds for the development of products based in technology, often in cooperation. At the time, Spain was the first or second, which was incredible because of all the competitors!

When I was told that they were relegating some Directors from their positions at CDTI and that the International Director was one of them, I knew I had to congratulate him on the work he had done. He could not go without at least having my appreciation. You do not know me, but one of the things that I have little confidence in are the politicians and the people related to their field, although I am aware that their work is important and that there are real heroes among them.

That being said, I asked my companions to give me José Manuel's name and email address in order to write him and express my gratitude as a citizen and a professional of innovation, which is what I did, symbolised in the book *Blue Ocean Strategy, Expanded Edition: How to Create Uncontested Market Space and Make the Competition Irrelevant*, authored by W. Chan Kim and Rene A. Mauborgne, which I handed over to José Manuel when we could finally meet.

This is how I met José. In response to that email he invited me to eat and we started a relationship where we would talk about innovation and ideas on how to improve the management of companies. Conversations in which he exuded passion and the desire to meet and learn more about other systems from other sources.

I suppose that is what unites us both, our passion for what we do. José Manuel stands out because of his public service, without self-interest, in which he combines his appetite for academic knowledge with the intrinsic nature of business and the companies he has been supporting and working for. It also helps that the presence of our company in Europe and the US gives us a lot of freedom to talk.

This book about innovation and entrepreneurship or, better said, about everything that he has been learning and experiencing in his professional career from the European Space Agency, CDTI, European Institute of Innovation and Technology and Red.es, offers us each a unique opportunity for reflection and learning. For the public sector it should be an obvious benchmark of comparison that hopefully will serve to improve future contexts and ecosystems.

I am not a person of great faith. I fled from the dogmas, groups, and corporations. I'm afraid of systems, institutions, rules. My hope and light are the people who struggle every day for what they believe in. The people who do their work with passion, who offer you affection without knowing you, who improve the moments you share with them. José Manuel is one of those people. In his field of innovation and service, his work is a light on the path that he shares selflessly.

Alfredo Sánchez

Madrid, December 2018

Afterword to the Spanish edition

by Totti Könnölä,
CEO of Insight Foresight Institute

If the reader has come this far, he or she has the sufficient perspective to read this epilogue with little doubt about the authority of José Manuel Leceta on the topic of innovation. However, it is not the only certainty you will have concluded. You also will have concluded that innovation fascinates him and that he does not stop from applying it to himself, hence his creativity. For this reason, although I could have written this epilogue recapitulating the topics that have already been discussed extensively throughout the book, I prefer to value the personal, fractal, and innovative contribution made by the author.

An epilogue refers to the speech, to the final part. It even projects a future ending that is yet to be written. Well, I would dare say that the author is already thinking about his next book in which he will undoubtedly incorporate a more philosophical and humanistic dimension, if possible, of which this work was inspired. Out of conviction and out of devotion, what experiences will you José Manuel share to enlighten us with your next book? I am already looking forward to reading it, to continue learning and, above all, to be surprised.

The fractality that gives title to this work makes sense to its full extent if we transcend the technological, scientific, productive, economic, and political dimensions associated with innovation. Areas in which Leceta operates with the fluency and mastery of one who knows these matters at a national and international level, as shown in the book. Innovation is his natural environment.

Rather than having his work be simply informative, it is impossible to avoid addressing the issues that he asks the reader to share with him, not only basic knowledge, but the passion to innovate, create, undertake, and experiment. In short, to dare. If this is the case, you will have empathised with the author from the beginning. The book could even be your accomplice. If this is not the case for the reader, at the very least just by touching the pages, the reader was inspired and was left with an enthusiasm for his or her profession. Furthermore, the author's generosity moves him to make the reader participate in the entire experience. We must thank him because a man of such sincere intellect made an effort to put black ink on white pages and share the lessons he has learned.

Returning to the content, the book shows that any technological innovation is also social innovation and, therefore, social changes are not just the reaction to technological change but an integral part of every successful innovation. They keep an ontological relationship that the author, far from shying away, incorporates into his vital "compass." In times of uncertainty and increasingly fluid changes, innovation is both the social and the personal solution. There is no Manichaeism between the technological and the philosophical, between the real and the virtual, between the material and the abstract. The important thing is the synthesis.

Following this dialectic, at IFI (Insight Foresight Institute), we share with the author the reflection that perhaps the innovation that is worthwhile, the one that is socially necessary and will be valued, will be the one that is least pending to invent solutions for problems that already exist but also anticipate new problems with the technology that are dormant and repressed under the pretext of social progress. Moreover, there are innovations that can generate socially undesirable consequences and if we want a better world, we must not let this happen.

Finally, I do not want to overlook something that permeates the entire book and stimulates us: the eclectic repertoire of quotes and references to other authors. It is not just an exercise of interdisciplinarity, it is an attitude that says it all.

Therefore, if we look to the future with confidence, with the attitude with which the author approaches it, the adventure of innovation will always be worth it.

Totti Könnölä

Madrid, October 2019

Epilogue to the English Edition

by **Dr. Josep M. Piqué**
Executive President at La Salle Technova,
II President of the Triple Helix Association
and XVII President of IASP,
and Prof. Jerome Engel
Founding Executive Director Emeritus, Lester Center
for Entrepreneurship- Haas School of Business,
University of California Berkeley.

Jose Manuel Leceta is a policymaker who, during his professional life, encouraged governmental leaders and public agencies managers to be key actors in shaping and nurturing innovation ecosystems. Understanding the nature of universities, industry, and government, Leceta developed several national and international policies whose positive impact we now recognize.

This book is a review of several works where Leceta was involved and the lessons that were learned in all the implementations. Reading this book, you will find the man behind the scenes, the person who was pushing, with knowledge, energy, and hope, several initiatives that we now enjoy. And the entire book is a big lesson: in every public or private initiative, there are people like Jose Manuel who are entrepreneurs, creating things that did not exist before and scaling and growing in a continuous learning process.

I thus believe that this book is a tribute to all the people who, like Leceta, had the opportunity to make a difference and took it, creating and promoting new activities that transformed previous realities and are now a legacy for future generations.

Thanks, Jose Manuel for your generosity and good will and for your public contributions during all this time.

If we had to summarise the book in 7 big takeaways, we would propose these:

1.- Triple Helix as a way of connecting ecosystems of innovation

With a Triple Helix perspective, Jose Manuel understood how important public policies were in providing the best environment at national and European levels. We can see at the national level the experience of CDTI, pushing international cooperation, transferring technology and co-developing common projects between countries, promoting the relationship of tech centres and companies for sharing and applying new solutions also from abroad.

On the other hand, also Universities and research centres, companies, and the government, as local Triple Helix agents, were connected with other Triple Helix agents to bridge technology between countries.

The government has the authority and the responsibility to promote ecosystems, but beyond that, Leceta with CDTI was bridging those ecosystems in a very smart strategy of collaboration: the diplomacy of innovation.

2.- Clusters of Innovation and the creation of Knowledge Innovation Triangle

But the real legacy of Jose Manuel Leceta was his leadership during the launch of the European Institute of Technology, EIT in Budapest. Inspired by MIT, the Massachusetts Institute of Technology, applying the best lessons of the USA, and understanding the assets and behaviours of Europe.

Leceta pushed forward the Knowledge Innovation Communities (KICs), promoting the relationship of technology-based entrepreneurs with investors and corporates. He created from scratch, in a European policy level, the collaboration between several co- location centres from all over Europe that were collaborating in the same KIC in a specific sector (like energy, climate change, ...).

The result of this work was a Cluster of Innovation at the European level with a specific specialisation in new venture creation, where talent and technology from universities and research centres create new high potential technology ventures and are connected with investors and incumbent corporations.

3.- Talent as the raw material of the knowledge-based economy

With the KICs, Leceta put the focus on the key asset of the knowledge-based economy: talent. With the purpose of activating brilliant talent, he promoted alliances between top Universities in Europe to share programmes for educating students to be tech-based entrepreneurs.

The outcome was not only positive in terms of numbers, but also in terms of how this young generation expected to exit the program: in addition to being a professor at the same university, they were challenged to be tech-based entrepreneurs, creating tech ventures with the potential for global scalability.

With this message, Leceta is shedding light on how the same talent could be promoted and encouraged to create their own jobs through EIT, and, better than that, to create quality jobs for others.

4.- Deep Tech for disrupting innovation

The future will be in the hands of whoever creates new technologies with impact. Challenges such as climate change, energy, food, health or mobility will need new technologies for changing the status quo, and moving forward democratisation of the technology. In the same way as Guttenberg with the printing revolution, and the

internet with the digital revolution changed the way of sharing knowledge and doing business, new technologies will change the future of energy, food, health or mobility.

Are the research centres ready for that? Leceta, with the KICs aggregates corporates and tech centres sharing the same challenges, trying to discover an iterative tech push – market pull dialogue for allowing new technologies to find applications and scalability, and for focusing the researchers in relevant needs for companies and markets.

Leceta with the KICs, teaches how Universities, Research and Technology centres could be more effective in the endeavour to transfer technology to society.

5.- Smart Finance from inception to exit plans

One of the key resources of the Clusters of Innovation is the capital— the smart money capable of financing in the appropriate way the needs of the entrepreneurs on their path to growth.

By connecting the KICs with the investor just at the beginning of the launching of new startups, Leceta was smart to understand that finance needs time and rules. And the rules of the game for the investors are clear in the different steps and in the evidence provided by the achievements of the team that is leading a new venture.

However, Leceta also connected investors with corporations through the KICS, allowing start-ups to visualise their exit plans through mergers and acquisitions of mature companies ready to absorb their business model.

6.- SuperClusters of Innovation as the path to grow for technology-based companies

With the Knowledge Innovation Communities – the KICs, Leceta implemented the Knowledge Innovation Triangle, connecting the best of the world of the Universities (talent coming from Education and Technology coming from Research) with the Corporates in different countries. The result was the construction of SuperClusters of Innovation combining Start Ups, Investors and Corporations in a pan-European level.

We can say that Leceta was a visionary in public policy, opening the door to Clusters of Innovation partnerships, including universities and research centres, entrepreneurs and corporates in a virtuous process of generating ecosystems of innovation in a pan-European approach.

With the KICs, Talent, Technology and Money were connected on a European level, crossing national boundaries with the flag of innovation, and connecting Europe with other Clusters of Innovation like Silicon Valley.

Intrinsic in the author's observations is the culture of innovation. That is to say simply and powerfully that having the elements (technology, talent and finance) are not sufficient to ignite the high velocity creation of a true SuperCluster of Innovation. The lubricant that enables these elements to combine and recombine in a self-reinforcing vortex of value creation is a culture that rewards behaviours that embrace a win-win approach. An approach that recognizes that a rising tide lifts all ships. This certainly does not mean the absence of competition, but enables an open innovation and entrepreneurial mindset that fosters collaboration to coexist with competition. It encourages business structures, such as shared ownership, that rely on incentives that align interests for mutual benefit, rather than prohibitions that constrain behaviour and punish violations.

7- The future (that we want) is about Leadership

The book provides different frameworks of Mind, Firms and Ecosystems. Leceta connects the different kinds of leadership (Artist, Athlete, Sage and Engineer) that we need in any organisation with the levels of innovation (Disruptive, Sustained, Radical and Incremental).

Leceta explains the importance of experience for doing and improving the implementation of new innovations. He underlines the opportunity and responsibility of individuals to create new things.

He highlights the fact that we are the future. That's what Jose Manuel Leceta has been

doing during his professional life as in agencies, serving society for a better future. Enjoy the book and the passion of Jose Manuel!

Josep M. Piqué
Barcelona, January 2023
and
Jerome Engel
San Rafael, January 2023

Acknowledgments

Like any worthwhile subject, this book is the result of a personal obsession to make innovation and entrepreneurship interesting for everyone. There is also a long list of people to whom I owe for helping me pursue what I am as well as who I would like to become.

First of all, I want to thank my peers and the public leaders of the Agencies where I have enjoyed so much throughout my career. Among them, I remember René Collette and his extraordinary team at ESA´s Directorate of satellite telecommunications. In CDTI, I received support and inspiration, not only from direct supervisors like José Enrique Roman, Emilia Buergo, and Maurici Lucena, but also from the whole Strategic Programmes team.

Later as CDTI International Director it was simply great working with extraordinarily talented people such as Javier García and Andrés Martinez, among many others. And at the EIT, I am indebted to a natural leader, Vasco de Janeiro, and the enviable auditor, Thomas Safrany for their generosity, with whom I was very close also by humble and idealistic origins. Finally, at Red.es, I worked with the best direction team and staff one could imagine, surrounded by professional examples such as Luis Palomo and Víctor Rodrigo.

This book has allowed me to once again meet with professionals like Alejandro Tosina and friends with whom I exchanged ideas and ended up signing many articles in the press. Among them,

Gonzalo León, my admired professor and PhD director; Maria Garaña, a top multinational executive, whom I met on the EIT Governing Board; Alfons Sauquet, also a member of the same board as Director of ESADE. Also, extraordinary peers like Angel Alba, founder of Innolandia, Senén Barros, President of the Red Emprendia and admirable educator and researcher at the University of Santiago in Spain. Also, Alex Coad, formerly at SPRU in the UK and CENTRUM PUCP in Perú, today at WASEDA Business School in Japan; Emma Fernandez, former corporate Director of INDRA and partner student at the Technical School of Telecommunication Engineering of Madrid from 1980 to 1987. Also, Totti Könnölä, a *rara avis* of scientific entrepreneur with whom I share many convictions and experiences.

I also thank with all my heart my wife Kremena and daughter Marina for sharing this journey together in trying to find ourselves along the way, as well as to do what each of us can do best for each other. After all, to choose one's attitude is the only thing we can control, as stoic Epictetus would say. At the same time, we should wish the best for those willing to work together and enrich ourselves while driving the boat that is our life into the way of improving the world around us.

I hope that the reader will excuse my insistence on the many paradoxes and dilemmas that ultimately characterise every human endeavour, because if innovation is essentially a journey to an economic discovery, I also believe that every worthwhile voyage turns out to be an inner journey. When we find the bumpy road, let us remember the sentence attributed to Seneca, the stoic of Hispanic origin: *Per Aspera Ad Astra,* "to the stars through difficulties."

Finally, many thanks to the Spanish journals *El País, El Mundo, Cinco Días* and *Expansión* for giving me permission to reproduce a large part of my articles that I first published in their newspapers. Also, to the Director of *TELOS* magazine, Juan Zafra, for his extraordinary editorial help with the former Spanish edition and to Pradja Paramita for proof reading the English translation.

Last but not least, my sincere gratitude to Martin Schuurmans and Maria Garaña for their incredible leadership and your words of introduction, as well as to Jerome Engel and Josep M. Pique for their thoughtful inspiration as per your concluding remarks to the English edition. To all four, congrats also for your exemplary contributions in academia and business, public and private.

BIBLIOGRAPHY

Audretsch, A. & Thurik, AR "A Model of the Entrepreneurial Economy", *International Journal of Entrepreneurship Education* 2 (2): 143--166, 2004.

Archibugi, D. & Michie, J. "The Globalization of Technology: A New Taxonomy", *Cambridge Journal of Economics*, Volume 19, Issue 1, 1 February 1995, Pages 121–140.

Archibugi, D. "Pavitt's Taxonomy Sixteen Years On: A Review Article", *Economics of Innovation and New Technology*, 10: 5, 415-425, 2001.

Baumol, WJ. *The Microtheory of Innovative Entrepreneurship*, Princeton University Press: New Jersey, US, 2010.

Blank, S. *The Four Steps to the Epiphany: Successful Strategies for Products that Win*, K&S Ranch Press, 2005.

Borras, S. & Edquist, C. *Holistic Innovation Policy: Theoretical Foundations, Policy Problems, and Instrument Choices*, Oxford University Press, 2019

Breznitz, D. *Innovation and the State: Political Choice and Strategies for Growth in Israel, Taiwan, and Ireland*, Yale University Press, 2011.

Christensen, C. *The Innovator Dilemma*, Harvard Business Review Press, 1997.

Coad, A., y Leceta, J. M. "Innovation and high-growth firms. Australian Innovation Report 2017". *Office of the Chief Scientist, Department of Industry, Innovation and Science, Australian Government*, 2017.

Cohen, WM & Levinthal, DA. "Absorptive Capacity: A New Perspective on Learning and Innovation", *Administrative Science Quarterly*, Vol. 35., 1990.

Diamandis, PH & Kotler, S. *Abundance: The Future is Better Than You Think*, Free Press, 2014.

Domingo, C. *El Viaje de la Innovación*, Deusto SA Ediciones, 2013.

Echeverría, Javier. *El Arte de Innovar*, Plaza y Valdés Editores, Madrid, 2017.

Engel, J. *Global Clusters of Innovation: Entrepreneurial Engines of Economic Growth Around the World*, Edward Elgar Publishing, 2014.

Fitjar, R. & Rodriguez-Pose, A. "Firm Collaboration and Modes of Innovation in Norway", *Working Paper Series in Economics and Social Sciences*, IMDEA Social Sciences Institute, 2011.

Freeman, C. *Technology Policy and Economic Performance*, London: Pinter, 1987.

Geels, FW. "Technological Transitions As Evolutionary Reconfiguration Processes: A Multi-Level Perspective and a Case-Study", *Research Policy* 31 (8/9), 1257–1274, 2002.

Geels FW & Schot, J. "Typology of Sociotechnical Transition Pathways", *Research Policy* 36, 399–417, 2007.

Hidalgo, A., León, G. & Pavón, J. *La Gestión de la Innovación y la Tecnología en las Organizaciones,* Ediciones Pirámide, Madrid, 2002.

Isenberg, D. *Worthless, Impossible and Stupid: How Contrarian Entrepreneurs Create and Capture Value Extraordinary,* Harvard Business Review Press, 2013.

Karo, E. & Kattel, R., 2015. "Innovation Bureaucracy: Does the Organization of Government Matter When Promoting Innovation?," *Papers in Innovation Studies 2015/38,* Lund University, CIRCLE - Center for Innovation, Research and Competences in the Learning Economy. 2015.

Kurzweil, R. *The Singularity is Near,* Lola Books, Berlin, 2012.

Leceta, J.M. & Könnölä, T. "EIT Digital: Leveraging Ecosystems for International Entrepreneurial Innovation", *Innovation: The European Journal of Social Science Research,* 2020.

Leceta, J. M., & Könnölä, T. "Fostering entrepreneurial innovation ecosystems: lessons learned from the European Institute of Innovation and Technology", *Innovation: The European Journal of Social Science Research,* 2019.

León, G., Leceta, J.M. & Tejero, A. "Impact of the EIT in the creation of an open educational system", *International Journal of Innovation Science,* 2018.

Leceta, J.M., Renda, A., Konnola, T. & Simonelli, A. *Unleashing Innovation and Entrepreneurship in Europe: People, Places and Policies,* CEPS Think Tank, Brussels, 2017.

Marías, J. *La Escuela de Madrid. Estudios de Filosofía Española,* Editorial Emecé, Buenos Aires 1959.

Mazzucato, M. *The Entrepreneurial State: Debunking Public vs. Private Sector Myths,* Anthem Press: London, 2013.

Molero, J. (coordinador) *Competencia y Cambio Tecnológico: un Desafío para la Economía Española,* Editorial Pirámide, 2000.

Molinuevo, JL. *Para Leer a Ortega,* Alianza Editorial, Madrid, 2002.

Ortega y Gasset, J. *El Tema de Nuestro Tiempo* Espasa Libros, Barcelona, 2003.

Pavitt, K. "Sectoral Patterns of Technical Change: Towards a Taxonomy and a Theory",

Research Policy, vol. 13, pp. 343-374, 1984.

Pérez, C. *Technological Revolutions and Financial Capital: The Dynamics of Bubbles and Golden Ages,* Edward Elgar Publishing, 2003.

Phelps, ES. *Mass Flourishing: How Grassroots Innovation Created Jobs, Challenge, and Change.* Princeton University Press: New Jersey, US, 2013.

Porter, M. *The Competitive Advantage of Nations,* Free Press, 1990.
Puig, M. *Reinventing Yourself,* Plataforma Editorial, 2012.

Rifkin, J. *The Third Industrial Revolution: How Lateral Power is Transforming Energy, the Economy and the World,* Palgrave Macmillan, 2011.

Thurik, AR. "Entrepreneurship, Economic Growth and Policy in Emerging Economies", *UNU-WIDER*, March 2009.

Van Stel, AJ. "COMPENDIA 2000.2: A Harmonized Data Set of Business Ownership Rates in 23 OECD Countries", *EIM Research Report H200302*, Zoetermeer: EIM Business and Policy Research, 2003.

Veugelers, R. "A Lifeline for Europe's Young Radical Innovators", *Bruegel Policy Brief*, Brussels, March 2009.

Von Neumann, J. *The Computer and the Brain*, Bon Ton, 1980.

Yergin, D. *The Quest: Energy, Security, and the Remaking of the Modern World*, Penguin Press, 2011.

World Economic Forum (WEF). *Enhancing Europe's Competitiveness: Fostering Innovation- Driven Entrepreneurship in Europe*, 2014. http://www3.weforum.org/docs/WEF_EuropeCompetitiveness_FosteringInnovat ionDrivenEntrepreneurship_Report_2014.pdf

World Economic Forum (WEF). *Collaborative Innovation: Transforming Business, Driving Growth*, 2015. http://www3.weforum.org/docs/WEF_Collaborative_Innovation_report_2015.pdf

BIOGRAPHY

PhD Telecommunication Engineer. Director General of the Ricardo Valle Innovation Institute Foundation (Innova IRV) in Malaga, Spain. Former Director General of Spanish Digital Transformation Agency Red.es from 2016 to 2018 and Director of the European Institute of Innovation and Technology (EIT) in Budapest, Hungary, from 2011 to 2015. Former International Director of the Center for the Development of Industrial Technology (CDTI) in Madrid from 2004 to 2010 and member of the Spanish delegation to the European Space Agency (ESA) since 1992.

Since January 2023 José Manuel is the Director General of the 'Ricardo Valle' Innovation Institute (Innova IRV), a private Foundation sponsored by AMETIC, the Spanish digital industry association based in Madrid. Innova IRV is a nation-wide initiative with international ambition aimed at catalysing the Spanish innovation system from the demand and needs of businesses and entrepreneurs.

Previously, he was Director General of Red.es, the Spanish Digital Transformation Agency from November 2016 to July 2018, where he renewed the organisation with a strategic plan, operational plans and innovative culture. Before that, following a competition at European level, Jose Manuel was appointed Director of the European Institute of Innovation and Technology (EIT) in 2011, shaping its first Knowledge and Innovation Communities (KIC) and inspiring early work on innovation models from KICs, which he then researched as a visiting fellow in the Robert Schumann Center for Advanced Interdisciplinary Studies at the European University Institute (EUI) in Florence, Italy.

Prior to joining EIT, he was International Director of CDTI, the Spanish National Innovation Agency, from 2004 to 2010, where he successfully increased the Spanish participation and leadership in the European Union R&D Framework Programmes by 50%. He also represented Spain at CREST-ERAC, Eureka and TAFTIE, an association of which he was the Executive Secretary in 2010. Last but not least, he expanded CDTI's Overseas Network with new delegations in India and the US, successfully launching bilateral technology co-development programmes with China, South Korea, Japan, India, South Africa and Canada.

Prior to that he had initially joined CDTI in 1992 as a member of the Spanish Delegation to the European Space Agency (ESA) in order to promote the role and leadership of Spain in the practical applications of space. He became Chief of the Department of Technology and Space Programmes at CDTI in 1996. Between 2000 and 2002, he was Chairman of the Ariane Programme Board and Vicechair of the Satellite Communications Programme Board at ESA. In addition, he played a key role in pioneering space initiatives,

ESA's water mission (SMOS), AMERHIS (the first digital multiplexer aboard a Hispasat satellite) and EGNOS-Galileo.

A PhD Telecommunications Engineer from the Technical University of Madrid, José Manuel also studied two years of Business Administration and graduated in Space Studies at the International Space University (ISU) Summer School in Toulouse, France in 1991; followed by Strategic Management of ICT, Telecommunications Economics, International Studies also in Madrid. He has university specialist degrees in Quantitative Research Methodologies as well as in Economics and Innovation Management. He started his career in Finland in 1987, working subsequently in the space industry in France, Spain, and Japan.

José Manuel is an international expert in strategies and policies for innovation and entrepreneurship. Co-author of *Unleashing report Innovation and Entrepreneurship in Europe : People, Places and Policies*, a report published in 2017 by the Brussels think tank CEPS, in 2021 he defended a doctoral thesis on the evolution of European policies for innovation and EIT: *Shifting Paradigms for European Innovation Policy: From Trans-National Collaborative Projects in R&D to Pan-European Entrepreneurial Ecosystems* including an empirical analysis of EIT Digital https://oa.upm.es/66440/ Since mid 2023 he is independent Board member of EIT Manufacturing and Chairman of the Innovation Commission at AMETIC, the Spanish national digital business association.

www.ingramcontent.com/pod-product-compliance
Lightning Source LLC
Chambersburg PA
CBHW031623210526
45464CB00004B/1720